APOLLONIUS OF TYANA
THE NAZARENE

APOLLONIUS OF TYANA

THE NAZARENE

DR. R. W. BERNARD

ANCIENT WISDOM PUBLICATIONS

WOODLAND, CALIFORNIA

Apollonius of Tyana the Nazarene
Dr. R. W. Bernard
Ancient Wisdom Publications
www.andras-nagy.com
ISBN-13: 978-1442102347
ISBN-10: 1442102349

Contents

Author's Foreword		7
Part 1:	The Historical Apollonius versus the Mythical Jesus	13
Part 2	Similarities between Apollonius and Jesus	29
Part 3	the Controversy	51
Part 4	Events in the life of Apollonius of Tyana	69
Part 5	Apollonius' Visit to the Brahman Sages of the Himalayas	77
Part 6	Apollonius Leaves Iarchus and Returns to Greece	89
Part 7	Labors of Apollonius in Greece	93
Part 8	Visit to the Gymnosophists	99
Part 9	the Trials of Apollonius by Nero and Domitan	105
Appendix	THE TREATISE OF EUSEBIUS	113

Author's Foreword

For over sixteen centuries, the Christian Church has been preaching its religion to the world. Yet when we consider the horrible events that have occurred among professedly Christian peoples during the recent world holocaust, resulting in the death of a significant portion of the world's population, we must conclude that there is something radically wrong with a religion, which, after having been preached and practiced for so many centuries, has led its followers to such a terrible state of affairs, involving the conversion of this planet into one vast slaughter-house, drenched in human blood, resulting from the mass murder of Christians of one nation by fellow-Christians of another, each being urged on and blessed by their own priests.

And such a condition has prevailed in Christiandom ever since the Christian religion was first created, organized and established in the year 325 A.D. by pagan Roman churchmen convening at the Council of Nicea. This council was presided over by the arch-murderer Constantine, Emperor of Rome, who had assassinated, in cold blood, a dozen of his near relatives, including his own wife.

And the history of Christianity has been no more honorable than its origin; for ever since Constantine first established it as the state religion of Rome, it has been responsible for the death of over fifty million innocent people, under the charge that they were "heretics," because they refused to accept the unreasonable dogmas of the church --including about three million women who were burnt alive as "witches" in comparatively recent times, by men who called themselves priests of the Christian religion.

What would the founder of Christianity, the gentle Nazarene and Prince of Peace, think of the crimes that have been perpetrated down through the centuries, in his name, by a church which professes to be his earthly representative -- the Church Militant! What would he think of the rotting corpses of over fifty million of his dearly loved brothers and sisters, who were put to death by this same church because they refused to accept its falsehoods and instead preferred to follow Truth, of which he was the great exponent?

And could a church whose Inguisition has left such a black record behind it be expected to offer us a written document (The New Testament) that could be accepted on face value as the authentic words of a man who taught peace, forgiveness and kindness, rather than bloody murder? And might it not be possible that not only the teachings but also the life history, and EVEN THE NAME, of the Nazarene, could, during the course of centuries, have been altered by the ecclesiastical scribes of the Church of Rome in the interests of its dogmas and ambitions for temporal power?

Also might not the original Nazarene, the peaceful Essene, whose goodness and pacifism extended not only to humanity but to the animal world as well, have been transformed, by Constantine's henchmen, the pagan Roman priests who became the Nicean Church Fathers, into another man -- called "Jesus Christ" -- more acceptable to their emperor? THAT THIS WAS THE CASE is the object of the following pages, devoted to the life and teachings of this unknown man, to prove.

Two thousand years ago a great teacher of humanity appeared in the world. He was a philosopher, a social leader, a moral teacher, a religious reformer and a healer. From one end of the Roman Empire to the other, wherever he went, divine honors were bestowed on him -- by all, from slave to emperor. He was undoubtedly the greatest man of his age; and his date of birth (4 B.C.) and period of activity coincided exactly with those of the Christian messiah, except that APOLLONIUS'S life of incessant labor in behalf of humanity extended for over a century, during which time he preserved his health of body and brilliance of mind unimpaired by the passage of time. He was a supreme exemplar of human perfection -- physically, mentally and spiritually. Oven seventeen temples were erected in honor of him in various parts of the Roman Empire. His name was APOLLONIUS OF TYANA.

No more courageous humanitarian and social revolutionist has ever come to this world to help the human race and redeem it from suffering. Alone and single-handed, he defied the bloodiest tyrants who ever sat on the Roman throne -- Nero and his more terrible successor, Domitian. Apollonius fearlessly traveled from one end of the Roman Empire to the other, inciting revolutions against the despots, and establishing communistic communities among his followers, who bore the name of Essenes, early Christians. And not content with such activities in the Roman provinces, he bravely entered Rome itself, after all philosophers had been expelled from the city under penalty of death by the cruel Domitian; there he openly denounced the tyrant, for which he was arrested and thrown into a dungeon, awaiting certain death which however, due to his brilliant speech in self-defense and his extraordinary powers of mind, he averted, securing his liberty.

Two centuries after Domitian, the arch-murderer and degenerate Constantine sat on the throne of Rome. While former Roman emperors hated Apollonius because of his revolutionary and "communistic" activities, Constantine especially hated his Pythagorean teachings -- his strict advocacy of vegetarianism, abstinence from alcohol and continence. Constantine enjoyed the red meats, the flowing wines and the beautiful women of his midnight revels too much to be willing to accept the religion of which Apollonius was the recognized head -- a religion which he imported from India, based on the doctrines of Chrishna and Buddha and bearing the name of Essenian Christosism.

It was for this reason that Constantine directed his armies to exterminate the descendants of Apollonius's Essenian followers, who were known as Manichaeans.

Finding that the religion of Rome was in a state of advanced decay and was daily losing hold on the masses, while the cult of Apollonius and the communistic communities of his Manichaean followers, in spite of the severest persecution, kept spreading, threatening the vested interests of Rome, Constantine's henchmen - the pagan priests of the Roman religion - decided to hold a convention at Nicea in the year 325 A.D., for the purpose of establishing a new religion. They decided to take over the popularity enjoyed by the followers of Apollonius, appropriate its essential doctrines (altering them so that they might be acceptable to Constantine), and to replace the philosopher Apollonius, whose abstemious Pythagoreanism was too well known and too much hated by their emperor, by a super-natural messiah whose teachings would be less radical and more acceptable to him.

So in place of Apollonius of Tyana, they put their newly created savior, whom they named "Jesus Christ," who, THEN AND THERE, was first conceived and created in the minds of Roman priests who were later known as the Nicean Church Fathers.

As soon as Jesus was put in the place of Apollonius, the task of the Roman churchmen was TO DESTROY ALL RECORDS concerning Apollonius and his Essenian Early Christian followers during the first three centuries, so that the world might forever be kept in darkness concerning this COLLOSAL DECEPTION, and be made to believe that Jesus and the Christian religion, which they originated at the BEGINNING OF THE FOURTH CENTURY A.D., antedated their creation by three centuries. It was for this reason that the Alexandrian and other ancient libraries were burnt, so that all books written during and pertaining to the

Apollonius of Tyana the Nazarene

FIRST THREE CENTURIES OF OUR ERA MIGHT BE DESTROYED.

And so well did the churchmen succeed in obliterating such records, that, for nearly two thousand years, the world has been kept in darkness concerning the fact that Apollonius of Tyana was the recognized world teacher of the first century, and that during the first three centuries, before he was created at the Council of Nicea, as an alternative messiah to Apollonius, no such man as Jesus Christ was known to or mentioned by ANYONE.

No greater cultural loss ever occurred than happened when the Christian mob set fire to the books and manuscripts of the Alexandrian Library, in order to destroy all records of Apollonius of Tyana, so that the world might forever be ignorant of his existence and of his replacement by the previously non-existent and unknown Jesus, which occurred at the Council of Nicea, in the year 325 A.D. But fortunately, a certain book survived - the FORBIDDEN BOOK - of all books in that great library - that was most feared. It was "THE LIFE OF APOLLONIUS OF TYANA", by his biographer, Philostratus. The book was secretly carried to the Near East for safety and for over a thousand years it was preserved among the Arabians, in spite of all efforts of the crusaders -- in the interest of the Papacy -- to destroy it.

Somewhat over four centuries ago, this forbidden book was first brought into Europe from the East; and it was not until 1801 that the first complete English translation, from the Latin, was made, in spite of the opposition of the clergy, who, when no longer able to suppress its publication, succeeded in rendering it oblivious and in maintaining the same popular ignorance of Apollonius and his historical significance as existed during the Dark Ages.

So well did they succeed, that, though while after the appearance of Blount's first English translation of Philostratus's biography of Apollonius at the commencement of the nineteenth century, his name was on every cultured Englishman's tongue; today, over a century later, he is almost completely unknown, even in academic circles, mention of him having been omitted from historical works and from the educational curricula -- so that, paradoxical though it may seem, the greatest man of the western world during the past two thousand years has been completely removed from the pages of history.

It is the purpose of this book to present the life and teachings of this man.

DR. R. W. BERNARD, B.A., M.A., PH.D. (1964)

Part 1: The Historical Apollonius versus the Mythical Jesus

In the year 325 A.D. was perpetrated one of the most collosal frauds and deceptions in the annals of history. This was the date of the Council of Nicea, whose task it was to create a new religion that would be acceptable to Emperor Constantine, who, at the time, was engaged in the bloody persecution of those communists and pacifists of ancient times who were known as early Christians. What made Constantine, in the midst of his inhuman massacre of these defenseless and despised people suddenly take over their religion and become its staunchest protagonist, is one of the enigmas of history which has never before been elucidated. On this point, Reville, a Catholic apologist; writes:

"The acknowledged triumph of Christianity during the reign of Constantine has always been considered one of the unaccountable revolutions and one of those historical surprises which, unconnected as they seem to be with any phenomena of the past might almost seem miraculous. One longs to find out by what process the human mind passes so rapidly from a contemptuous and utter denial of the teachings of Christianity to an interest and avowed sympathy for the doctrines of the new creed...It was in the fourth century, immediately after the most violent persecutions, that Christianity, though embraced and professed by a minority only, succeeded in attaining to a commanding position in matters both social and political."

Aware that the old religion of Rome was in a state of advanced decay and was daily losing its hold on the people, while the persecuted cult of the Essenes, or early Christians, in spite of all the efforts to suppress it through the most bloody and inhuman means, continued to thrive and win the increasing respect of the masses, the Church Fathers, themselves previously pagans whose hands were stained with the blood of those from whom they stole their religion, saw that by adopting Christianity (in a revised form) they could take advantage of the popular prestige created by the martyrdom of the early Christian saints, and at the same time win the support of Constantine, who, in being converted to the Christian faith, could cover up his own past crimes, gain increased public favor and extend and consolidate his empire.

In order to make the previously despised cult of the Essenes, or early Christians, acceptable to Constantine, emperor of Rome - the Church Fathers had to remove from its teachings certain doctrines which they knew were objectionable to him. Chief among these was the prohibition against the use of meats and wines, which was a cardinal doctrine of early Essene Christianity. It was for this reason that the churchmen at Nicea found it necessary to remove from the Gospels these objectionable doctrines, for they knew that Constantine loved the red meats and flowing wines of his midnight revels too much to be willing to accept a religion which required from its adherents complete abstinence from these indulgences, as early Essene Christianity did. To accomplish this, certain "correctors" were appointed, whose task it was to rewrite the Gospels, omitting all that pertained to vegetarianism and abstinence from alcohol. The Church Fathers had an additional reason to do this - for they themselves had no desire to make such a radical change in their own living habits.

That the original Gospels were rewritten and altered at the Council of Nicea is indicated by the following statement by Archdeacon Wilberforce, who writes:

"Some are not aware that, after the Council of Nicea, A.D. 325, the manuscripts of the New Testament were considerably tampered with. Prof. Nestle, in his 'Introduction to the Textual Criticism of the Greek Testament,'

tells us that certain scholars, called 'correctores,' were appointed by the ecclesiastical authorities, and actually commissioned to correct the text of the Scripture in the interest of what was considered orthodoxy."

Commenting on this statement, Rev. G. J. Ouseley, in his "Gospel of the Holy Twelve," writes:

"What these 'correctores' did was to cut out of the Gospels with minute care, certain teachings of our Lord which they did not propose to follow -- namely, those against the eating of flesh and taking of strong drink -- and everything which might serve as an argument against Flesh eating, such as the accounts of our Lord's interference on several occasions, to same animals from ill-treatment."

There is evidence to indicate that not only were the original doctrines of early Essene Christianity radically changed at the Council of Nicea and replaced by others entirely different, but that the MAN whose life was an embodiment of the original doctrines was likewise replaced by another man who exemplified the new doctrines. The name of the second man, who was not a vegetarian and who did not prohibit the killing of animals, was Jesus Christ, who was put in the place of Apollonius of Tyana, the historical world teacher of the first century.

The first act of the Church Fathers, after they created their new religion and its messiah, neither of which existed previously, was to burn all books they could lay their hands on, especially those written during the first few centuries, which made no mention of Jesus and which referred to Apollonius as the spiritual leader of the first century, realizing as they did that such books, if they were not destroyed, constituted a dangerous menace to the survival of their deception. It was for this reason that the churchmen took such great pains to burn the ancient libraries, including the famous Alexandrian Library with its 400,000 volumes, which was burnt to the ground by edict of Theodosius, when a Christian mob destroyed the

Serapeum where the scrolls and manuscripts were kept.

However, the churchmen failed to their purpose, for prior to its burning which they foresaw, the librarians of the Alexandrian Library had secretly removed from it some of the most precious volumes, which they carried eastward for safety.

Among the works which were thus saved from the flames of the Alexandrian Library, the one which has created the most widespread and long-continued discussion was the "Life of Apollonius of Tyana," written by Flavius Philostratus at the beginning of the third century A.D. As if by irony fate, this book - which of all books burnt in the Alexandrian Library, was one of the most dangerous - was preserved down through the centuries, resisting all attempts to destroy it. The reason why this book was so much dreaded by the churchmen was because, while it made no mention whatsoever of the existence of Jesus or of Christianity, it presented Apollonius of Tyana as the universally acclaimed world teacher of the first century, reverenced from one end of the Roman Empire to the other, by everyone, from the lowest slave to the Emperor himself.

No book ever written has aroused by heated argument over a longer period of time than this biography by Philostratus. From the early centuries of our era, when Hercules and Eusebius first started it, until the days of Blount, Voltaire and the Deists, the controversy raged unabated. For Philostratus, in his book described a character, born in the very year of the birth of Christ, who, in every respect, was the equal, if not the superior, of the Christian messiah.

W. B. Wallace, writing on "The Apollonius of Philostratus," calls Philostratus's biography a "pagan counterblast to the gospel of Galilee, representing a Greek saviour as an alternative to the Semitic one." (Westminster Review, July-Dec. 1902). Furthermore, the main events of the lives of both men were so closely parallel that the reader cannot help but conclude that if Jesus is not a fictitious imitation of Apollonius, then Apollonius must be an imitation of him, since it would be highly improbable for two such similar men to have been born the same year and to have such similar biographies.

F. A. Campbell, in his 'Apollonius of Tyana,' writes:

"The birth of Apollonius is assigned to the year 4 B.C. But as everybody knows, the current computation of the beginning of the Christian era is incorrect, and the first year of our Lord ought to be dated four or five years earlier. If the Apollonian and Christian nativities both belong to the same year, the coincidence is entitled the more attention than it has received."

"Thankful Tyana, like ungrateful Nazareth, had nursed a prophet of blameless life, of miraculous power, of super-abundant loving-kindness, and of heroic virtue. Both Apollonius of Tyana and Jesus of Nazareth were born in the same lustrum, if not the same year. Both Tyana's babe and Bethlehem's were said to have sprung from a divine Father and a human mother, and both of these holy ones drew their first breath amid gracious portents and supernatural singings. Nor were these the only parallels in the memoirs of the Tyanean and the Nazarene.

"Orthodox Christians had been accustomed to affirm boldly the finality of Mary's son; but, like a bolt from the blue, here was Philostratus opposing himself to Matthew, Mark, Luke and John and offering an alternative Messiah."

Also it is strange that, though they were both supposed to be the greatest men of their age, they did not know of each other's existence. And since there is absolutely authentic historical evidence of the existence of Apollonius, but not a shred of genuine proof of the existence of Jesus, we must conclude that if one of these figures is fictitious and an imitation of the other, it is Jesus who is the fiction and Apollonius the historical personage. Concerning the existence, or rather, the non-existence, of Jesus, Tschendorf writes:

"Author after author, volume after volume, of the life of Christ may appear until the archives of the universe are filled, and yet all we have of the life of Jesus is to be found in Matthew's gospel. Not a single person specially associated with Jesus impinges history."

In Taylor's "Diegesis," [1829, Oaknam, England] we read:

"We have investigated the claims of every document possessing a plausible claim to be investigated which history has preserved of the transactions of the First century and not so much as a single passage, purporting to have been written at any time within the first hundred years, can be produced to show the existence of such a man as Jesus Christ or of such a set of men as could be accounted to be his disciples."

Commenting on this statement by Taylor, J. M. Roberts, in his "Antiquity Unveiled," [1892; Oriental Publishing Co., Philadelphia] writes:

"On the other hand we have abundant proof that Jesus Christ is founded on the known life of Apollonius of Tyana, the earthly existence of whom has never been questioned, to which added passages from the lives of various personages, and teachings are concerning the mythical gods of other lands. The Prometheus of the Greeks was the character which suggested the crucifixion (also the crucifixion of Chrishna in Christosite traditions.) The Eleusinian mysteries suggested the "Last Supper" and these together with doctrines of ancient sun worship were gathered and represented to be a history of the events connected with the life of the Christian Jesus. (Prometheus on the crag, suffering for the good of mankind, suggests Jesus on the cross, changing Prometheus for Jesus and the Sythian crag for the cross.)

"In the first chapter of Matthew the geneology of Jesus is given as the twenty-eighth generation from David down through Joseph to Christ. In the third chapter of Luke the same geneology is given as being the forty-third generation from Christ through Joseph to David. This is a very remarkable oversight on the part of the translators, for if there was anything they could *agree on, it is in regard to the descent of Christ.*

"All the Christians that ever lived or ever will live will find their ideal Jesus but a phantom -- a myth. They can chase it as a child would a butterfly through a meadow on a summer's afternoon, and it will elude their grasp. The Christian Jesus is nothing more than the Chrishna of the Hindus."

No contemporary writers who lived at the time when Jesus is supposed to have lived make mention of him; though forged allusions to Jesus occur in the books of Livy and Josephus. In his "History of the Jews," written in the First century, at a time when Jesus would have enjoyed his greatest popularity among the Jews if he had existed, though pages and pages are devoted to persons of no importance whatever and who would have been forgotten forever had not Josephus mentioned them, there is not a single mention of Jesus in the original edition. On this point, Dr. Edmond B. Szekely, in his "Origin of Christianity, writes:

"There is not a word, or better, there is no longer a word in the works of Flavius Josephus about the Messiah, the Christ crucified by Pontius Pilate, except for a crude interpolation, quite obviously false...The silence of Josephus is not due to disdain or studied neutrality."

In an eighth century Slavonic edition of Josephus's book, such an interpolation occurs, referring to a certain Jesus, son of Joseph, and which covers only a passing paragraph, the brevity of which clearly reveals its fraudulent origin, for, if Jesus were mentioned at all, much more space would have been devoted to him. And coincident with such interpolations of early authors, occurred the censorship of all books making reference to Apollonius, whose name was omitted or abbreviated. (Thus, in the original Pauline Epistles, which, we have reason to believe, originally had Apollonius as their central figure and were written by him, his name is abbreviated to "Apollos" and "Pol" (Paul.)

That Apollos (conceded by no less an authority than the Encyclopedia

Britannica to be an abbreviation of Apollonius) was the real author of the Epistle to the Hebrews, falsely attributed to Paul, was the opinion of Martin Luther and other eminent scholars.

And if Apollonius wrote some of the so-called Pauline Epistles, there is a possibility that he may have written others, AND, IN FACT, ALL).

Plutarch, the eminent biographer, who lived between 46 and 120 A.D. would certainly have made mention of Jesus if he had existed, since he wrote when Jesus's fame would have been at its height. Yet in the voluminous works of Plutarch, not a single reference to any such man as Jesus can be found. Although Plutarch's miscellaneous writings make mention of or allude with unerring certainty to nearly every religious and ethical opinion of his time, he is absolutely silent on the subject of Christianity and concerning the existence of Jesus. Though he knew the utmost detail of the lives of great men who lived centuries ago, we could hardly believe that Plutarch could have been entirely unaware of the existence of such a great man as Jesus who lived only a few years previously. This is all the more surprising because the provinces of Bithynia and Pontus, where Plutarch lived, were only a few days' journey from Boetia, where, if we may believe Christian writers, the proselytes of Christianity were swarming at the time.

But while Plutarch belonged to a different race and was born after his alleged crucifixion, Philo, a Jew, who lived at exactly the same time in the first part of the first century, and who visited the Essenes and wrote about them, should, and above all others, have made mention of Jesus, who, if he had lived, would undoubtedly have been the leader of this sect. Yet not one word is found in Philo's writings concerning the existence of Jesus, any more than is there one word in the original edition of the "History of the Jews" of Josephus. Nor did any other writer in the first century mention Jesus. They did not because he did not yet exist. He was first born three centuries later, created by the churchmen at Nicea, in their effort to find an alternative messiah, more pleasing to Constantine and the Romans, to be put in the place of Apollonius.

That the early Christians themselves, and not only the Pagans, were ignorant of the existence of any such man as Jesus, has been clearly proven by the catacomb researches of Eisler, a student of early Christian archaeology. In his work, "Orpheus the Fisher," Eisler shows that no representations can be found among the catacomb inscriptions that depict Jesus, the cross or the crucifixion. Instead, a Greek figure is represented as the leader of the sect, a vegetarian and friend of animals, depicted either under the fig - of Orpheus playing his lyre and surrounded by friendly animals, or as the Good Shepherd (Hermes) carrying a lamb around his neck. These representations obviously refer to Apollonius whose cardinal teachings consisted of vegetarianism and the abolition of animal sacrifices. Eisler's findings were further verified by Lundy, who, in his "Monumental Christianity," a work on early Christian archaeology, likewise reports the entire absence of any reference in the catacomb inscriptions to Jesus or a crucified saviour, in whose place is found the familiar Greek figures of Orpheus and the Good Shepherd, who are represented as friends of animals.

The closest original that can be found of the Jesus of the New Testament is a rabbi named Jehoshua Ben Pandira, who lived about a century B. C. In his "Life of Jehoshua," Dr. Franz Hartman states that this illegitimate child of a Jewish maiden, Stada, and a Roman soldier, Pandira, who is mentioned in the Talmud, was the original Jesus. He was referred to as a rabbi of not very great importance, who studied the mysteries in Egypt, and who was put to death by stoning after an attempted crucifixion.

Seeking a substitute for Apollonius, the Church fathers seized upon Jehoshua, and changing his name to that of the Druid sun god, HESUS, and shifting the date of his birth forward a century, he was transformed into Jesus. On this subject, Manly Hall writes: "It is very possible that the early Church Fathers, seeking desperately for a concrete human being on which to hang the fabric of their faith, picked Jehoshua Ben Pandira as the nearest parallel to be found among the Jewish rabbins. Armed with this small fragment of history, they proceeded to correlate the two; building in a little here; and removing same contradictory fragment there, until, lo, and behold, the 'King of Kings' is a Nazarene, in spite of the popular opinion that nothing good can come out of Nazareth.

"This Further explains why Helena, the mother of Constantine, within three hundred years after the death of Jesus, was unable to find in all of Jewry any man who had even heard of him. According to the story, she finally came upon one aged man who claimed to have heard that Jesus had lived. He took her to an old Roman execution field where the excavation revealed a number of crosses. When the whole matter had been settled to every one's satisfaction, Constantine, to show his extreme veneration, had one of the passion nails pounded into a bit for his horse.

"The most perplexing and comparatively unsolved mystery with which the Christian theologian is faced is the almost complete lack of historical evidence concerning the life of Christ. If we accept a few palpable forgeries, our knowledge of the life of Christ is based principally upon the accounts given in the Gospels... The gravest doubts exist as to the authorship of the gospels of the New Testament. The Encyclopedia Brittannica acknowledges not only these doubts, but admits that there is no proof of any kind that the Gospels were written by the men whose names have been affixed to them in more recent time."

In 1894, there appeared a remarkable book written by J. M. Roberts entitled "Antiquity Unveiled," in which evidence was presented to prove that no such man as Jesus of Nazareth ever lived, but the name was adopted by the framers of Christianity to cover the identity of Apollonius of Tyana whose teachings and mode of life they purloined and made use of as a model upon which to construct their system." He adds: "The world has the uncontrovertible testimony that Christianity is of spurious origin and the most consummate piece of plagiarism in human history."

In sharp contrast with the scarcity, or rather the absence of information regarding Jesus, is the abundance of reliable historical data available concerning Apollonius of Tyana, who, during the first century, enjoyed universal fame from one end of the Roman empire to the other, being honored by all. More than seventeen temples were dedicated to him in various parts of the empire. Nearly a dozen Roman Emperors held him in awe and reverence. (The Roman emperors; Vespasian, Titus and Nerva, were all, prior to their elevation to the throne, friends and admirers of Apollonius, while Nero and Domitian regarded the philosopher with dismay.) The Emperor Septimus Severus (A.D. 193-211 erected a statue to him in his gallery of deities in the Pantheon, while his son, Emperor Caracella, honored his memory with a chapel or monument.

Lampridus, who lived in the third century, further informs us that the Emperor Alexander Severus (A. D. 222-235) placed a statue of Apollonius in his labarium side by side with one of Orpheus.

It was the wife of Septimus Severus, the empress Julia Domna who commissioned the philosopher, Philostratus, a member of a circle of writers who collected around her, to write the life of Apollonius of Tyana, based on manuscripts in her possession, chiefly the memoirs of Apollonius's disciple and traveling companion, Damis, in addition to records preserved in different cities where Apollonius was held in esteem -- from temples whose long-disused rite he restored, from traditions, from epistles of Apollonius addressed to kings and sophists and from his letters -- of which the Emperor Hadrian had made a collection which he deposited in his palace at Antium. (Julia Domna, known as the philosopher-empress because she was surrounded by men of letters and philosophers and dispensed enlightened patronage to thought and learning, was the daughter of Bassiamus, priest of the sun at Emesa in Syria. Philostratus was a member of a group of famous writers and thinkers who gathered around her. She was a woman of high intelligence and remarkable purity of character, living in seclusion and devoting her time to literature and philosophy in her extensive library. As in the case of Sappho, a woman of egually exemplary morality, she was falsely defamed by the scribes of the same churchmen who were later responsible for the brutal murder of Hypatia. These three greatest women of antiquity, together with Joan of Arc, the greatest woman of modern times, were all victims of a criminally jealous male clerical fraternity.

Another biography of Apollonius was written by Soterichur of Oasis during the reign of Diocletian, but is non-existent, having been destroyed by the Christians together with other ancient writings referring to him. Still another biography was written by Moeragenes, which was likewise lost.

Though written in the early part of the third century A.D., Philostratus's biography of Apollonius of Tyana was not permitted to be publish.ed in Europe until the year 1501, when Aldus printed the first Latin edition to appear in Europe. This was followed by an Italian and French translation, but it was not until 1680 that the first English translation was made by Blount, an English Deist.

Blount's notes on the book raised such an outcry that, in 1693, the book was condemned by the church and its further publication forbidden. (Concerning the effects of Blount's translation; Campbell, in his "Apollonius of Tyana," writes: "Fierce passions were let loose. Sermons, pamphlets and volumes descended upon the presumptious

Blount like fireballs and hailstones and his adversaries did not rest until the authorities had forbidden him to print the remaining six books of his translation.")

In his notes, Blount pointed out that, "we must either admit the truth of the miracles of Apollonius as well as those of Jesus, or, if the former were untrue, there would be no better ground to believe in the latter." A century later Blount's notes were translated into French by the Encyclopedists. However, a century before Blount - Voltaire, Le Grand d'Aussy, Castillon and other French Deists wrote to the same effect, considering Apollonius as a far more authentic historical figure than Jesus, and fully his equal in every respect and as worthy of performing miracles if such were possible. (Francis Bacon also spoke of Apollonius in the highest terms. In Burton's "Anatomy of Melancholy" - which some have attributed to Bacon's authorship - appeared a quotation from Philostratus's biography of Apollonius to which Keats later referred in a footnote in his "Lamia.")

Blount, however, had translated only the first two books of Philostratus's work (there were eight in all, the remaining six remaining unpublished); and it was not until 1809 that the first complete English version was made by Edward Herwick. (In his preface of his work entitled "The First Two Books of Philostratus Concerning the Life of Apollonius to which Tyaneus, written originally in Greek, and now published in English," Blount, in self-protection, and obviously expressing opinions the opposite of what he really believed, humbly described his book as "no more than a bare narrative of the life of a philosopher, not of a new Messiah, or any ways in opposition to the old; no, Philostratus does not anywhere so much as mention the name of Christ. And if one Heathen Writer (Heirocles) did make an ill sue of this history, by comparing Apollonius with Christ, what is that to Philostratus, who never meant nor designed it so, as I can anywhere find? However Eusebius hath already confuted Hierocles, which confutation I had intended to have annexed to Philostratus as an antidote."

"The whole translation I have already finished, and had proceeded thus far as you see in my illustration, when I found the alarm was given in all parts what a Dangerous Hook was coming out; such a book as would unmask all practical atheists, which (they being the greater number of men, might therefore prove of pernicious consequence to the public. Above all, the Popish Clergy thought themselves chiefly concerned herein, who are so zealously revengeful and malicious, that I feared it is might fare with me as it did with poor Esop, (who notwithstanding he had broken jests upon several great kings and potentates without being punished for the same, yet only speaking against the priests of Delphos cost him his life.)

"Wherefore, if the Clergy would have Apollonius esteemed a Rogue and a Juggler, that being risen from the dead, he is one of the principal fomenters of this Popish Plot; or that there never was any such man as Apollonius, with all my heart, what they please. For I had much rather have him decried in his reputation than that some grave Cardinal, with his long beard, and his excommunicative 'Ha', should have me burnt for a heretic.")

Herwick's volume became so rare that in 1907, two London book dealers of world-wide reputation searched and even advertised in vain for a copy. This indicates how well the ecclesiastical suppression of this dreaded book had succeeded. And while today scarcely a person can be found, even among the most educated, who even heard the name of Apollonius of Tyana, much less knew anything about him, according to Campbell, "There was a day when the name of Philostratus and Apollonius of Tyana was on every educated Englishman's tongue," even though sectarian prejudice against Apollonius characterizes every writer prior to the nineteenth century. The popularity of Apollonius in ancient times stands in sharp contrast to his almost complete oblivion today.

That Apollonius, a mere man, should rival Jesus, a god, in so many important respects, in the eyes of the churchmen constituted an important reason to suppress Philostratus's book, since it tended to belittle the dignity of their savior. That Philostratus composed his "Life of Apollonius of Tyana" as a pagan counterblast to the Christian gospels is an opinion which has been held by reputable scholars both before and after Blount's day. (This opinion, which has been widely held by Christian writers, is evidently false, since Christianity as we know it did not exist at the time when Philostratus wrote, for he makes no mention of Jesus or of Christianity. In spite of this fact, the book has always been held with the greatest suspicion; and, even after the Renaissance, when it was introduced into Europe, Aldus hesitated for a time before he gave the right to publish it, at last resolving to do so, but adding to the text a reply by Eusebius to Hierocles' criticism of Christianity, in which he opposed the Apollonian to the Christian miracles, thereby, as he expressed it, giving "the antidote with the poison.")

Thus, the Bishop of Avranches, writing in the seventeenth century, expressed this view as follows: "Philostratus seems to have made it his chief aim to deprecate both the Christian faith and Christian doctrine, both of which were progressing wonderfully at that time, by the exhibition on the opposite side of that shallow representation of a miraculous science, holiness and virtue. He invented a character in imitation of Christ, and introduced almost all the incidents in the life of Jesus Christ into the history of Apollonius, in order that the pagans might have no cause to envy the Christians by doing which he inadvertently enhanced the glory of Christ, for by falsely attributing to another the real character of the Savior, he gave to the latter the praise which is His just due, and indirectly held Him up as the admiration and praise of others."

Tredwell, in his "Sketch of the Life of Apollonius of Tyana," writes:

"From the time that disputes began concerning the Christian religion, Christians have charged Philostratus with having appropriated the events and miracles contained in Matthew's gospel to adorn his life of Apollonius of Tyana, and the pagans have made countercharges of plagiarism against the writer of this gospel. Upon the earlier accounts of Apollonius these charges have been held to be of sufficient importance to meet with efforts of refutation from eminent Christians; even as late as our day, Rev. Albert Reville did not think it beneath his dignity nor his great learning, to attempt in 1866 a refutation of 'this great and monstrous infidel slander.' He attempted to show in a little book bearing the title of 'Apollonius the Pagan Christ of the Third Century' (meaning the first century) that Philostratus had borrowed leading facts from the Gospel of Matthew. Miraculous phenomena were related almost identical with that record by Matthew in his gospel of Jesus Christ. And while Jesus is said to have been casting out devils in Galilee, Apollonius was, according to a tradition quite as trustworthy, rendering mankind a similar service in Greece. Such was the opinion of Catholic writers on the subject; and, according to Daniel Huet, this statement by the Bishop of Avranches 'ever since that time has had great weight with all thoughtful minds.'"

Part 2 *Similarities between Apollonius and Jesus*

Let us now consider some of the essential points of similarity between the biographies of Apollonius and Jesus. Before his birth, the coming of Apollonius was preceded by an Annunciation, his coming being announced to his mother by an Archangel. He was born in the same mysterious manner in the same year when Jesus is supposed to have been born (the year 4 B.C.) Like the latter, in his childhood he displayed wonderful precocity in religious matters; then he went through a period of preparation; then came a period of public and positive activity; then a passion; then a kind of resurrection; and finally an ascension.

The messengers of Apollo sang at his birth as the angels did at that of Jesus. He also was exposed to the attacks of enemies, though always engaged in doing good. He similarly went from place to place carrying out the work of reform, being accompanied by his favorite disciples, amongst whom disaffection, discouragement and even treachery made their appearance. And when the hour of danger was at hand, in spite of the prudent advice of friends, and the abandonment of his disciples, he went straight to Rome, where Domitian, the cruel emperor, was seeking to kill him, just as Jesus went up to Jerusalem and to certain death. And before this event, he had been a victim of Domitian's no less cruel predecessor, Nero, as Jesus had been exposed to the machinations of Herod Antipus. Like Jesus, he is accused of working miracles of mercy by the aid of magic and unlawful arts, whereas he only succeeded in working them because he was a friend of the gods and worthy to be esteemed as such. Like Jesus on the road to Damascus, he fills an avowed enemy with wondering dismay by an apparition several years after his resurrection and ascension.

Another remarkable resemblance between Apollonius and Jesus was the great number of cases of evil spirits that were driven out at his bidding. He speaks to them, as it was said of Jesus, with authority. The young man of Athens, who was possessed, through whom the devil uttered cries of fear and rage, and who could not face the look of Apollonius, reminds us of the Gospel narrative of the demoniac of Gadera. Neither was cured until some outward visible circumstance had taken place that gave the people reason to believe that the devil had really gone out. In the one case a herd of swine rushed down into the lake, and in the other a statue falls, overthrown by the violence of the evil spirit as it rushes out of the young man.

There is also mentioned in the biography of Apollonius another case of possession singularly like the one of the epileptic child in the three first gospels. In Rome, Apollonius restored a young girl to life under circumstances which immediately remind us of the return to life of the daughter of Jairus. It may be further remarked that both stories are so recorded that a careful critic might ask himself with respect to each whether the young girl who was brought to life again had really been dead after all. The lame, the blind and the halt came in crowds to be healed by the laying on of hands by Iarchus, the chief of the Brahman sages of the Himalayan heights whom Apollonius visited and under whom he studied and derived his knowledge and power.

His miraculous appearance to his friends - Damis and Demetrius - who thought at first that he was a spirit, remind us at once, in the way this was related, of the resurrection of Jesus after his death.

The following inspiring description of the Christ-like figure of Apollonius is given by Campbell in his book, "Apollonius of Tyana:" "A strange distinctive figure, clad in white linen and not in garments wrought of skins; with feet unsandled and with locks unshorn; austere, reserved, and of meagre mien; with-eyes cast upon the ground as was his manner, Apollonius of Tyana drew to him with something of a saint's attraction all simple folk, and yet won as intimates the Emperors of Rome.

"*Through his love for all life and swift appreciation of the beauty of the human form, he drew high to the sufferings of the body and became acquainted with the sufferings of the soul. He sought to heal, or at least to soothe, some of the distresses, physical and spiritual, of poor humanity; and to such a singular degree of skillfulness did he attain in the healing arts of his day, that even the sacred oracles of Agaea and of Delphi pronounced him more than mortal, referred the distempered body and the smitten soul to him, for relief, knowing that from his very presence proceeded a peculiar virtue, a benign influence an almost theurigic power.*

"*By years of silence and contemplation, by extensive travel and by a continuous spiritual and worldly experience, he deepened to no minute measure, an originally, powerful. and intense personality, and so it was that at length he became the admiration not only of all countries through which he passed, but of the whole Roman and Hellenic world. Cities sent envoys and embassies to him decreeing him public favors; monarchs bestowed special dignities upon him, counting him worthy to be their counsellor; incense was burnt before his altars; and after his death divine honours were paid to his images, which had been erected, with great enthusiasm, in all the temples of the gods. Nor did his fame evanesce. All down the ages his name has carried in it something of a hurricane; for speculative critics of both early and later days have thought to find in the life of this exceptional character a parallel to the life of Christ, and to ground an argument thereon, against the supernal claims of the Son of Man. Hence for centuries even the name of Apollonius wag odious to Christians; for it seemed the very Gospel of the Son of Man was at stake; and Christian apologists, on their* part, in self-defense, were not lacking to attack fiercely their adversaries' champion, and to denounce him as little better than an imposter, a sorcerer and a magician; on this account they have generally failed to understand the man. They have lacked, at least in their combative approach to him, that sweet affection for signal worth, that gracious patience for nobleness, which is absolutely essential to comprehend a new or startling character or mode of life."

Another writer gives the following description of Apollonius:

"He had a Zeus-like head, long beard and hair descending to his shoulders, bound with a deep fillet. Damis describes Apollonius as ever mild, gentle and modest, and in this manner, more like an Indian than a Greek, though, when witnessing some special enormity, he would burst out indignantly against it. His mood was often pensive, and when not speaking he would remain for long with eyes cast down, plunged in deep thought. Though always stern with himself, he readily made excuses for others. As an instance of this, the following may be cited: During Nero's reign, when, on his way to Rome, Apollonius was warned that he and his followers would be in danger, of thirty-four companions who set out with him, only eight remained staunch enough to brave the threatened peril; while praising the courage of those few who remained with him, he refused to blame as cowards the many who had fled."

From Phliostratus's biography, we gather the following facts about the life and character of Apollonius of Tyana. He was born in the year 4 B.C. At the age of twelve he was sent to Tarsus in Cilcia, the alleged birthplace and home of "St. Paul." There he studied every system of philosophy, and perfected himself in rhetoric and general literature. He took up residence in the temple of Aescalupius, famed for its marvelous cures, and was initiated by its priests into their mysteries, after which he performed cures that astonished not only the people but those masters of the art of healing. He then finally decided to adopt the philosophy of Pythagoras, and rigorously observed the trying discipline instituted by the Samian sage. He abstained from animal food, wine and women -- and lived upon fruits and herbs, dressed only in white linen garments of the plainest construction, went barefooted and with uncovered head, and wore his hair and beard uncut. He was especially distinguished for his beauty, his genial bearing, his uniform love and kindness, and his imperturbable equanimity of temper.

In these respects he was the personal embodiment of the imaginary traits of the Christian Jesus, and was no doubt the original of the pictures of the so-called Nazarene, now so venerated by the uninformed professors of the Christian religion. (Almost every picture that in modern times is recognized as a likeness of Jesus really have their origins in a portrait of Apollonius of Tyana painted in the reign of Vespasian.)

Determined to devote himself to the pursuit of knowledge and the teaching of philosophy, he gave away his large patrimony to his poor relatives and went to Antioch, then a center of learning but little less noted than Athens or Alexandria. There he began his great mission by teaching philosophy to a number of disciples and to the people. He then entered the temple of Apollo Daphne at Antioch and learned the mysteries of its priests. Later he traveled to India in search of wisdom and visited the Gymnosophist philosophers of Egypt. He then returned to Greece to restore the Mysteries and to teach the doctrines of Chrishna and Buddha, which he learned at the feet of his Himalayan teacher, Iarchus. (These Teachings, embodying the Buddhist gospels that Apollonius carried westward, became the origin of the Christian religion).

As a a social and political reformer, he traveled from one end of the Roman Empire to the other, inciting revolt against the cruel tyrants - Nero and Domitian, for which he was arrested by both and thrown into jail.

After his arrest by Domitian he was acquitted and "disappeared." After having completed his labors for humanity which lasted a century, it is believed he went to India to rejoin his teachers in the Himalayas. When and where he died is unknown.

Ells gives the following account of the life of Apollonius:

"He was born in Tyana, A Greek City of Asia Minor, three years before the birth of Christ, and he lived about a hundred years, until the reign of Nerva. As with Moses, no man knoweth his grave unto this day. Devoted to philosophy from his boyhood, he studied it after the unequalled method of those days, by listening to lectures and to disputations of rival thinkers in every market-place and from the steps of every temple. He chose as his own the philosophy of Pythagoras, and enthusiastically practised its austerities, maintaining absolute silence for five years as a mental discipline, avoiding all relations with women, giving away his patrimony, and wearing only linen [cotton] garments.

"In the phraseology of today he was a vegetarian and a total abstainer. He claimed that by this mode of life his senses were made abnormally acute, so that he had a premonition of future events and became aware of the minds of men and of distant happenings; and he successfully set up that defense when he was tried for 'sorcery' before the emperor. He prayed to the Sun three times a day, offering incense but never sacrificing victims. He believed in the immortality of the soul, in metempsychosis [reincarnation], and in a supreme diety - the Creator of the Universe. Indeed it may be argued that in the deities whom he worshipped he saw merely phases and agencies of this Supreme Deity, for in referring to the gods collectively he is frequently quoted by Philostratus as using indiscriminately the words 'gods' or 'god,' and the Indian sage Iarchus, with his evident approval, likens the Universe to a ship of which the Creator is the Master and the subordinate 'gods' are petty officers [cf. the Christian idea of orders of 'angels' who *assist in the smooth running of creation, and the Hindu idea of a trinity of 'gods' - Brahma, Vishnu and Shiva - representing the creative, preserving and destructive energies that are operating continually within the creation, each having their correlative functions or energy centers (chakras) within the human body - which in itself is but a microcosm or reflection of the macrocosmic universe.]*

"All his life long his advice and help were constantly sought by cities, temples and rulers everywhere, and were freely given without reward. He journeyed over the known world from the Atlantic ocean to the Ganges river, and south to the cataracts of the Nile, acquiring and imparting wisdom. In middle age, when his travels were not half completed, he told his disciples that he had already seen more of the earth's surface than any other man had ever done. During his long and laborious life he wrought many wonders, and many men regarded him as an incarnate divinity. The kings of Persia and of India vied with each other to do him honor. After his death the Emperor Hadrian built a temple and endowed a priesthood for his worship of Tyana. The emperor Aurelian vowed to do the like, calling him the most godlike, holy and venerable of mankind, endowed with more than mortal powers, and declaring: "If I live, I will publish at least a summary of his wonderful deeds, not because they need anything my words can give, but to make them familiar to all lips, as they are marvelous."

"Another emperor, Alexander Severus, with questionable taste, set the image of Apollonius in his private chapel or solarium, among his tutelary deities, in company with Orpheus, Abraham and Christ (Though this reference has been quoted by many writers, it appears very improbable that early Roman emperors, prior to Constantine, who was the first to accept Christianity, had statues of Abraham or Christ in their chapels. This statement is obviously a Christian interpolation. [forgery] The statue of Orpheus is the only one we can believe to have existed side by side with that of Apollonius. *As Eisler has shown, even in the Catacombs of the early Christians there was no representation of Jesus, while Orpheus is represented as the central object of Worship. It is probable that Orpheus was considered as the founder of the religion of which Apollonius was the apostle.)*

This very history we owe to the reverence paid to his memory by the empress Julia Domna, the wife of Septimius Severus, who commissioned Philostratus to write it and supplied him with most of the materials. For two hundred years after his death, Apollonius was generally acclaimed as more divine than human, until in the reign of Diocletian a Roman proconsul Hierocles attempted to sweep back the rising tide of Christianity by publishing his "Candid Words to Christians," in which he drew unfavorable comparison of Christ with Apollonius. The nascent church easily confuted his attack, but could not forget nor forgive it; and not content with its victory over its assailant, it stigmatized the long-dead philosopher as a charlatan inspired and aided by the devil.

The chorus of destruction has been very persistent. As late as the time of Charles II, when one Charles Blount tried to publish in England a translation of Philostratus' biography, he complains in his preface that the clergy would only let him print the first two of its eight books, and that the Catholic priesthood was especially active in its opposition. (Eells, C.P., "Life and Times of Apollonius of Tyana.")

Since ancient times, the controversy raged between the followers of Apollonius and those of Jesus as to who was the more highly moral type. The partisans of Apollonius argued that he, being a man, offered humanity a more useful moral example than Jesus, a god, who could only be worshipped, but not imitated, and in comparison with whom Apollonius was as virtuous in every respect, and in some ways more so. They pointed out in particular, that a man who, from his sixteenth year, resolved to live only on fruits and herbs and to remain forever chaste

-- which resolution he strictly followed throughout his long life of over a century -- was certainly a higher and more moral type than one who sat and ate among publicans the viands offered him and who drank wine at wedding feasts.

Already at the beginning of the fourth century A.D., Hierocles wrote a treatise in which he maintained that Apollonius was a much higher type than the Jesus of the Gospels. Hot controversies ensued on the subject; and the Catholic opponents of Apollonius invented the most ridiculous lies to belittle his character. Thus Arnobius and the fathers of the church, just after its formation at the beginning of the fourth century, maliciously attributed the reputed miracles of Apollonius to magic, while putting up a fictitious imitation of him in the form of the messiah of their new religion. Even as late as the fifteenth century, we find Pico della Mirandola, and as late as the sixteenth century, Jean Bodin and Baronius, still denouncing Apollonius as an evil magician who had a pact with Satan.

However, even the enemies of Apollonius had to admit that his life was exemplary, for here was a man who, from a tender age, resolved to abstain from meat, from wine and from association with women, who let his hair grow long and did not permit a blade to touch his chin, and who also as a Pythagorean naturist, went around bare footed or wore sandals made from bark, not from leather, dressing only in white linen robe and considering it an impurity to wear clothing made from the wool of sheep.

Spending his time in a temple, his silence was extraordinary, yet his knowledge of languages was universal. From one end of the Roman Empire to the other he traveled as a teacher and healer, to whom the sick flocked wherever he went. He was also a social reformer and revolutionist, who fearlessly opposed tyrants, inciting uprisings against them, and organizing his followers into communistic communities.

It thus appears that Apollonius was a much higher moral, as well as intellectual type than the humble carpenter of Galilee. Such considerations have led Reville, a Catholic writer, in his book on Apollonius of Tyana, to admit, "Jesus was only the offering of an obscure people; his doctrine was but the refinement of a paltry local tradition; his life, of which little is known the great majority of his contemporaries, was extremely short. He soon fell victim to the attacks of two or three priests, a petty king, and a prosecutor, and a few remarkable progidies alone distinguished him from a crowd of other existences which had nothing whatever to do with the destinies of humanity.

"*Apollonius, on the contrary, a Greek by birth, had stored his vast intellect with the religious doctrines of the whole world, from India to Spain; his life extended. over a century. Like a luminous meteor he traversed the universe, in constant intercourse with kings and the powerful ones of the earth, who venerate and fear him, and if he ever meets with opposition, he triumphs over it majestically, always stronger than his tyrants, never subject to humiliation, never brought into contact with public executioners.*

Tredwell, in his "Sketch of the Life of Apollonius of Tyana," writes as follows:

"*That Apollonius was a great and good man can hardly be questioned; the tribute paid him by Titus, Vespasian and Aurelius is a guarantee. Even among those of the present day most willing to detract from his character many are forced to admit that a certain pure and true morality pervades the whole of his system of teaching. There is a well- established theory in it, that virtue and true piety is the only foundation of happiness.*

"*Apollonius was chaste and temperate; he was actuated by a noble desire to know and the still nobler desire to communicate his knowledge to mankind. He was ingenious, learned and original in his language. No man ever lived who utterly rejected all vulgar artifice for producing effect upon men; no majestical pomp of words characterised his teachings. And he was ready at all times and in all places to impart good instruction; and from all testimony of him no man was more emphatically an apostle of peace. It is difficult, indeed, to overcome the common-sense conclusion that Apollonius, whom Philostratus has placed before us, is a real man, a corporeity, and not a spirit; he walks the earth, eats, drinks and sleeps like other men, loves and hates as experience teaches us is natural for man. He is an observer of natural phenomena, compares and speculates, adores nature, birds, animals, trees, flowers and is not destitute of humor, although of great gravity and dignity. Everywhere in nature and art, with the Brahmans of India, he found something to admire."*

Towards the end of the third century, just previous to the formation of the church, the struggle between the Pythagorean supporters of Apollonius and his opponents, who later organized the Roman Catholic Church at Nicea, reached its last and bitter stages . At this time there were temples and shrines all over Asia Minor dedicated to Apollonius and his work, but there were none to Jesus, for he was unknown since he did not exist.

In the place of the august Apollonius, whose fame was world wide during the first three centuries, and who was revered in all centers of learning as the wisest of men, his opponents endeavored to set up an uneducated youth of only local significance, who was known only to a few illiterate fishermen in his vicinity, and whose short period of activity (3 years) and his short life (33 years) precluded his achieving what Apollonius with his century of incessant activity had accomplished. While Jesus spent his life in Galilee among the common people, Apollonius traveled from one end of the world to the other, studying the wisdom of the greatest minds that could be found -- the Brahmans of the Himalayas, the Gymnosophist philosophers of Egypt, and Druids of Gaul, etc.

According to Tredwell, Apollonius travelled more extensively than any man of his age. "That he was a man of no mean account," Tredwell adds, "is evident from his letters addressed to kings, rulers, philosophers societies and the first men of his time, still extant, reserved in the works of Philostratus and Cujacius. He traveled among the Magi and was everywhere the more honored on account of his modesty and virtues; giving always wise and prudent counsel, and rarely disputing with anyone. The prayer which he was accustomed to offer up to the gods is admirable. "O, ye immortal gods, grant us whatever you shall judge it fit and proper to bestow, and of which we may not be undeserving."

For many centuries after his passing, a halo of sanctity was thrown around his head, and he was worshipped as a god in many parts of the world. The Tyanaeans elevated him to the position of a demigod, and the Roman emperors approved his apotheosis. But in the course of time, the deification of Apollonius showed the same fate as that decreed the Roman emperors; and his chapel became as deserted at that which the Athenians erected in honor to Socrates.

It was claimed for Apollonius by his followers that he was the son of a god (Proteus), a claim which he repudiated. Nevertheless it was believed by people that Apollonius was of divine parentage and that messengers of Apollo sang at his birth. Ammonianus Marcellinus ranked Apollonius among the most eminent men, and claimed that he prophesied by supernatural aid of a genius, as did Socrates and Numa.

The miracles said to have been performed in India by the Hindu savior, Chrishna, during his mission being almost identical with those attributed to Apollonius, were all well known and discussed in Alexandria at this time; and although Apollonius never encouraged the propagation of his divine nature, yet he never emphatically repudiated it, knowing that but little respect attached to the person or teachings of any philosophy with the vulgar multitudes unless founded on evidence of divine inspiration, the demonstrations of which were in the form of "miracles," and he appears to have allowed the vulgar populace to believe this. Thus arose the belief that he was the son of God, and was a second Chrishna, or a Christ.

Out of respect to Apollonius, his native birthplace of Tyana was regarded as a sacred city and was exempted from the jurisdiction of governors sent from Rome. Gibbon, in his history of Rome, states that a superstitious reverence of the countrymen of Apolloniua caused the emperor Claudius Aurelian (A. D. 273) to treat with lenity the conquered city of Tyana.* (*That in spite of his eminence as a historian of Rome, Gibbon was ignorant of the true significance of Apollonius, is indicated by the following statement of his: "We are at a loss to discover whether Apollonius was a sage, an impostor or a fanatic." In view of such ignorance by an outstanding authority on Roman history, we can well imagine how the general public were uninformed on the subject at the time that Gibbon wrote, as it still is.)

Vopiscus writes that as the forces of Aurelian were marching against Tyana, the citizens having shut the gates against him, incensed the emperor so that he declared that he would not leave a dog alive in the city; but the spirit of Apollonius appeared to him in his tent, threatened him into a better mind, and for Apollonius's sake, he spared the inhabitants. Later he dedicated a temple in his honor, as the emperor Marcus Aurelius also did. The emperor Hadrian, with reverent pomp, deposited Apollonius's writings in his splendid palace at Antium, whither pilgrims flocked daily in crowds to see them.

Apollonius's reputation as a saint was so well established during the early centuries that even after the advent of Christianity, many Christian writers, including Cassiodorus, spoke highly in his praise. Lactantius says that a statue of Apollonius was erected at Ephesus. Statues were erected to him in the temples and divine honors were paid him by the Emperors

Caracella, Alexander Severus and Aurelain, while magical virtues were attributed to his name. Newman claims that Apollonius was everywhere hailed as a god, and when he entered a city made converts as soon as seen. This was the case in Olympia, where the crowds paid more attention to him than to the games, almost worshipping him.

At Ephesus, he was worshipped under the title of Hercules, the warder-off of evil. Reville says that "after his death, the city of Tyana paid him divine honours; and the universal respect in which he was held by the whole of the Pagan world testified to the deep impression which the life of this supernatural being had let indelibly fixed in their minds, an impression which caused one of his contemporaries to exclaim, "we had a god living among us."*

(*Newman, a Catholic apologist, first seeking to discredit Apollonius and then admitting his greatness, writes: "Apollonius is represented as making converts as soon as seen. It was not then his display of marvels, but his Pythagorean dress and mysterious deportment, which arrested attention, and made him thought superior to other men, because he was different from them. Like Lucian's Alexander, he was skilled in medicine, professed to be favored by Aesculapius, pretended to foreknowledge; was in collusion with the heathen priests, and was supported by the Oracles; and being more strict in conduct than Paphlagonian, he established a more lasting celebrity.")

After Apollonius's passing, for centuries he received from emperors honors equal to those which they claimed for themselves, and he was universally deified and worshipped as a demi-god. Philostratus writes that "the country people say he was a son of Zeus, but he claims to be the son of Apollo, as his name indicates. Apollonius has been called the "true friend of the gods." Pierre Bayle, in "Dictionaire Historique et Critique" (1696), remarks that Apollonius was worshipped in the beginning of the fourth century under the name of Hercules, and refers for his authority to Vopiscus, Eusebius and Marcellinus. Albert Reville says, "The universal respect in which he was held by the whole pagan world testified to the deep impression which the life of this supernatural being had indelibly fixed in their minds."

Philostratus speaks of a temple in Tyana dedicated to his memory and founded at the imperial expense, "for the emperors had judged him not unworthy of like honors with themselves." It was from the priests of this temple, who had gathered as much information as they could about Apollonius, that Philostratus got much of the material for his biography.

Concerning Apollonius's universal renown during the first century, W.B. Wallace writes: "His noble countenance, his winning presence, his pure doctrine, his unsullied life, his ardent advocacy of the immortality of the soul, as well as his miracles - led men to believe, wherever he went, that he was more than mortal. He consorted and corresponded with the mighty ones of the earth. (J.A. Froude writes: According to Philostratus he was a heathen saviour, who claimed a commission from heaven to teach a pure and reformed religion, and in attestation of his authority went about healing the sick, curing the blind, raising the dead men to life, casting out demons, stilling tempests, and prophesying future events - which came afterwards to pass.

"He was born four gears before the Christian era in Tyana, a city of Cappadocia. His parents sent him to be educated at Tarsus, in Cilicia, a place of considerable wealth and repute, and he must have been about the beginning of his studies when St. Paul as a little boy was first running about the streets. On the death of his father, he divided his property among the poor, and after five years retirement he traveled as far as India in search of knowledge. Here he discoursed with the learned Brahmans, and came home with enlightened ideas. He began his career as a teacher in the

Roman Empire. He preached his new religion and performed miracles to induce people to believe in him. He was spiritual advisor of Vespasian. By Domitian he was charged with having pretended being a god himself. He was arraigned, convicted and was about to suffer, when he vanished out of the hands of the Roman police and reappeared at Ephesus... Apollonius of Tyana, among many others, was looked upon as an emanation of the divine nature. --(J. A. Froude, in "Nineteenth Century," Sept. 1879.)

Tigellinius, the brutal favorite of Nero, cowered before him, Vespasian was encouraged by him to aim at the Imperial diadem. His disciples were numerous.* (*On this point, Mead, in his "Apollonius of Tyana," writes: "He attracted to himself many followers and disciples. It would have been interesting if Philostratus had told us more about these 'Apollonians,' as they were called, and whether they constituted a distinct school, or whether they were grouped together in communities on the Pythagorean model, or whether they were simply independent students attracted to the most commanding personality of the times in the domain of philosophy.")

Indicating the high reverence in which Apollonius was held in his day, Justin Martyr, in his work written in the second quarter of the first century, made the following statement:

"Question 24: If God is the maker and master of creation, how do the consecrated objects of Apollonius have power in the (various) orders of creation? For, as we see, they check the fury of the waves and the power of the winds and the inroads of vermin and attacks of wild beasts."

The followers of Apollonius, who were called Apollonians, continued to worship him until the fourth century. Many of them wore the same dress as himself and adopted his Pythagorean vegetarian mode of living.* (*However, Apollonius never imposed his mode of life on others, even on his personal disciples, whom he gave utmost freedom. Thus, he tells Damis that he has no wish to prohibit him from eating flesh and drinking wine, though he demands the right to refrain himself and of defending his conduct if called to do so. This is an indication that Damis, who was the source of Philostratus's information concerning the life and teachings of Apollonius, was not a member of the inner circle of discipline, and therefore was not in a position to communicate as much about his master as he otherwise would have been able to do.

In the Pauline Epistles, which, in their original form, were undoubtedly written by Apollonius, Damis is referred to as "Demas,"** a companion of the apostle (Paul, or Pol, representing Apollonius, who also appears in the epistles as "Apollos," who is said to have preached a similar doctrine and in a similar manner as Paul.***)

[** Colossians Chapter 4: Verse 14; 2nd Timothy, Chapter 4: Verse 10; Philemon: Verse 24.]

[*** I Corinthians, Chapter 3: Verses 4 - 6; also Verse 22; I Corinthians, Chapter 4: Verse 6; Titus, Chapter 3: Verse 13.]

Admitting that he was not permitted to enter the inner circle of his teacher and master, Damis refers to his manuscript on the "Life, Journeyings and sayings of Apollonius of Tyana," which later came into the possession of Julia Domna, who obtained it from a relative of Damis, and which constituted the basis of Philostratus's biography, as "the crumbs of the feast of the gods." Repeated mention is made of their accompanying Apollonius on his travels, sometimes as many as ten of them at the same time, but none of them were allowed to address each other until they had fulfilled the vow of silence. The most distinguished of his followers were Musonius, who was considered the greatest philosopher of the time after Apollonius, and who was the special victim of Nero's cruelty, and Demetrius, 'who loved Apollonius' as his master.

These names are well known to history; of names otherwise unknown are the Egyptian Dioscorides, who was left behind owing to weak health on the long journey to Ethiopia; Menippus, whom he had freed from an obsession; Phaedimus and Nilus, who joined him from the Gymnosophists; and of course Damis, who would have us think that he was always with him from the time of their first meeting at Ninus.

There is reason to think that the followers of Apollonius were Essenes or Therapeuts, of which sects he was undoubtedly the leader. According to Reville, "Apollonius and his followers, like Pythagoras and his disciples, constituted a regular order of Pagan monks."

Lecky, in his well known book, "History of European Morals," states that Apollonius "obtained a measure of success second only to that of Christ.* (*Renan called Apollonius "a sort of Christ of paganism." Reville calls him a Greek or Pagan Christ, "a universal priest, a philosopher who is so holy as entitled to divine honors," and "a god in human form". "He advocated a morality and virtue far in advance of the religious sentiments of his age." Again he writes: "Apollonius of Tyana, at the close of the Flavian period, endeavored, with noble purpose, to unite moral training with religious practice; the oracles, which had long ceased, were partially restored."*

(*According to Phillimore, Apollonius founded a church and a community, composed of his disciples - who were undoubtedly the branch of Essenes known as Nazarenes or Therapeuts. Phillimore says, "Apollonius may be said to have founded a 'church;' but there was nothing commercial in the institution; he was not salaried by his admiring disciples."

It appears that Apollonius was himself an object of worship -- because of his sanctity, wisdom, beauty, etc. - wherever he went. "His magic powers, which seem to have been considerable, procured for local piety his recognition as an object of cultus in his Cappadocian birth-place," writes Phillimore. There is evidence that Apollonius's "church," whose adherents were known as "Apolloniei" survived for some centuries after his death, and constituted the origin of what, after the Council of Nicea, was later transformed into he Christian Church.)

G.R.S. Mead, a student of early Christian and Gnostic movements, writes along similar lines as follows: "Apollonius of Tyana was the most famous philosopher of the Graeco-Roman world of the first century, and devoted the major part of his long life to the purification of the many cults of the Empire and to the instruction of the ministers and priests of its religions. With the exception of Christ no more interesting personage appears upon the stage of western history in these early years."

Appuleis classes Apollonius with Moses and Zoroaster, and other famous prophets and magi of antiquity. Arnobius, the teacher of Lactantius, at the end of the third century, also classes him among the great prophets, side by side with Zoroaster. But while the previous universal high opinion of Apollonius was lost after the formation of the Church, the Church fathers were not all of the same mind concerning him, for on the one hand we find John Chrysostom bitterly denouncing Apollonius as a deceiver and evil-doer, Jerome asserts that the philosopher found everywhere something to learn and something whereby he could become a better man. Also in the next century, St. Augustine, while ridiculing the attempts that were made at comparison with Jesus, admits that the character of Apollonius was exemplary in virtue.

Vopiscus, a writer who lived at the end of the third century, is very enthusiastic about Apollonius, whom he called "a sage of the most widespread renown and authority, an ancient philosopher and a true friend of the gods, indeed, a manifestation of Deity." Vopiscus resolved to write a life of Apollonius in Latin, so that, he says, "his deeds and words may be on the tongues of all, for as yet the only accounts are in Greek. For who among men," he adds, "was more holy, more worthy of reverence, more venerable and more god-like than he?" He it was who gave life to the dead. He it was who did and said so many things beyond the power of men.

Vopiscus did not fulfill his intention, but Soterichus, an Egyptian epic poet of the last decade of the third century, Nichomachus, and Tascius Victorianus all wrote lives of Apollonius, which were lost after the formation of the Church, having been destroyed by the Christians.

During the fifth century, we find Volusian, a pro-consul of Africa, descended from an old Roman family, still worshipping Apollonius of Tyana as a supernatural being. Lactantius refers to a statue erected to him at Ephesus. Sidonius Apolinaris, who wrote his biography in the last half of the fifth century, speaks of him as the favorite of monarchs and the admiration of the countries he traversed. This same writer sent a copy of Philostratus's "Life of Apollonius of Tyana" to his friend, Leo, the chancellor of a Frankish king at Toulouse, with this message:

"Throw aside your endless labors and steal a respite from the burdens and bustle of the Court, so that you may really study this long-expected volume as it deserves. When once absorbed in it, you will wander with our Tyanean over Caucasus and Indus, to Brahmans of India and the naked philosophers of Nubia. It describes the life of very much such a man as you are, with due respect to your Catholic faith. Courted by sovereigns, but never courting them; eager For knowledge; aloof from money-getting; fasting at feasts; linen-clad among wearers of purple; rebuking luxury; self-contained; plain-spoken; shock-headed in the midst of perfumed kings, who themselves were reeking with myrrh and malo-bathrum and polished with pumice-stone; taking from the flocks nothing to eat or to wear; and notwithstanding all these peculiarities not distrusted but honored wherever he went throughout the world, and although royal treasures were placed at his disposal, accepted from them merely those gifts to his friends which

it suited him better to bestow than to receive. In short, if we measure and weigh realities, no philosopher's biography equal to this has ever appeared in the times of our ancestors; so far as I know; and I am certain that in my times it finds a worthy reader in you."

Other references to Apollonius were derived from a certain Machus, the unusual color of whose robes won him the name of Porphyry, who wrote a celebrated treatise against Christianity which was destroyed by the Emperor, but his life of Pythagoras and his school, written in the last years of the third century and the first years of the fourth, is still in existence, as is also a similar work by Iamblichus written at the same time; and both refer to Apollonius's biography of Pythagoras, the first thirty sections of which constituted the course of their information.

Tredwell says that there was a vast amount of literature produced during the Apollonian period, "more probable than was ever produced during a like period by the like number of persons. All we know about it is, that it once existed and was destroyed during the subsequent ages. It was obviously burnt by the Christians."

Apollonius was a man of extensive learning and the author of many books, all of which have been destroyed by the Christians.* (*Apollonius was the author of the following books:

(1) "The Mystic Rites or Concerning Sacrifices." This treatise as mentioned by Philostratus, who tells us that it sets down the proper method of sacrifice to every god, the proper hours of prayer and offering. It was in wide circulation, and Philostratus had come across copies of it in the libraries and cities, and in the libraries of philosophers. Several fragments have been preserved and have been found in the writings of Eusebius. Noack tells us that scholarship is convinced of the genuineness of this book, which was widely circulated and held in the highest respect. It is said that its rules were engraved on brazen pillars at Byzantium, which were melted down by the Christians.

(2) Four books entitled "The Oracles or Concerning Divination." According to Philostratus, the Full title was "Divination of the Stars," and he says that it was based on what Apollonius learned in India; but the kind of divination Apollonius wrote about was not the ordinary astrology, but something which Philostratus considers superior to ordinary human art in such matters. He had, however, never heard of anyone possessing a copy of this rare book.

(3) "The Life of Pythagoras." Porphyry refers to this book, and Iamblicus quotes a long passage from it.

(4) "The Will of Apollonius." This was written in the Ionic dialect, and contained a summary of his doctrines.

(5) "A Hymn to Memory." (Eudocia speaks of many other works, all of which, including the ones above described, were destroyed by the churchmen.) He was familiar with Plato, Pythagoras, Livy and Horace, as indicated by his frequent quotations from them; but his favorite author was Homer, and his philosophy was the dialectic stoicism of Zeno. He was the author of four books on Judicial Astrology and a treatise on Sacrifice, referred to by Eusebius and Suidas.

The Emperor Hadrian had a book he had written which he kept with his letters in his palace at Antium. According to Tredwell, it seems probably that Apollonius was the author of a voluminous literature, much of which Philostratus must have had before him in a diary of Damis. Marcus Aurelius (A.D. 130) learned stoic philosophy from Apollonius's writings. "From Apollonius," said Aurelius, "I have learned freedom of will and understanding, steadiness of purpose, and to look to nothing else, not even for a moment, except to reason."

Part 3   the Controversy between Adherents of Apollonius and Jesus

Let us briefly review the history of the controversy between the adherents of Apollonius and those of Jesus, each of whom claimed that the miracles of their messiah were greater than those of the other.*

(*On this subject, Mead writes: "The development of the Jesus-Apollonius-miracle controversy into the Jesus-against-Apollonius and even Christ-against- Anti-Christ battle, fought out with relays of lusty champions on the one side against a feeble protest at best on the other, is a painful spectacle to contemplate. How sadly must Jesus and Apollonius have looked upon, and still look upon, this bitter and useless strife over their saintly persons? Why should posterity set their memories one against the other? Did they oppose one another in life? Did even their biographers do so after their deaths? Why then could not the controversy have ceased with Eusebius? The answer to these questions is clear to the reader of this book.")

It started in the early part of the fourth century with the publication of Hierocles' "Lover of Truth," which was refuted by Eusebius in a work entitled, "The Treatise of Eusebius, the Son of Pamphilis, Against the Life of Apollonius of Tyana" Written by Philostratus, Occasioned by the Parallel Drawn by Hierocles between him and Christ." Hierocles' book was an attack on Christianity, charging the Christians of CREATING Jesus as a plagiarism of Apollonius, a charge that STILL HOLDS GOOD, since it has NEVER BEEN REFUTED. On this subject, Roberts writes:

"All through the third century there is repeated mention of this (Apollonius's teachings). But it was not until Hierocles in the beginning of the fourth century boldly charged upon the Christian priesthood their plagiarism of the teachings and works of Apollonius, that the latter found it necessary to set every means at work that could in any way help to conceal the great truth that Hierocles proclaimed with such portentious force. It was true that no one knows exactly what it was that Hierocles wrote, for Eusebius, who took upon himself the task of destroying the testimony of Hierocles, took precious good care to destroy the work of his formidable opponent, and give his OWN VERSION of the matter instead. The reply of Eusebius to Hierocles has come down to us. Why has not Hierocles' arraignments of the Christian priesthood also come down to us? Let that priesthood answer."* (* J. M. Roberts -"Antiquity Unveiled.")

In refutation of Hierocles' claims, Eusebius tried to show that Apollonius was a poor imitation of the Christian messiah. On the other hand, Hierocles, insofar as this can be gathered from Eusebius's refutation -- made the following statements:

"You proclaim Jesus a god on account of a few progidies recorded by their evangelists, yet we have writers of more education than yours and with more care for truth, who relate solid judgement, do not make him a god on account of them, only regard him as a man found pleasing to the gods."

This is practically all that Eusebius tells us about the contents of the work of Hierocles under the title of "Philalethes." Everything else, in the book, he asserts, has been urged by others and has been already replied to. The parallel between Apollonius and Christ is all that is new. Eusebius examines each of Philostratus' eight books in succession, pointing out the inconsistencies and incredibilities of the narrative. "I have no objection," he says, "to placing Apollonius as high as any one likes among philosophers. But when, under the cover of Pythagoreanism, Philostratus makes him go beyond the bounds of philosophy and makes him a saint, he is really made to be an ass in lion skin, a juggling quack instead of a philosopher. There are limits set to human powers which no man, like Apollonius, can transgress, but a higher being (Jesus) can condescend to the conditions of human nature."

In short, Eusebius mocks Apollonius's miracles as untrue and impossible and tries to point out the inconsistencies of the biography, concluding that if the miracles of Apollonius really took place they were performed by the aid of a demon.

"Lastly," says Eusebius; arriving at the culmination of his argument, "Philostratus, having thrown doubt on the place and manner of his departure from life, will have it that Apollonius went to heaven bodily, accompanied by an expected song of maiden voices."

Eusebius ends by saying that if any should think fit to place Apollonius among philosophers, he does not object; if only they will clear him of the false ornaments affixed to him by the writing under examination; the real effect of such additions being to culminate the man himself under the guise of raising him to divinity. In conclusion let us hear Eusebius's own words:

"I need not say with what admiring approval he [Hierocles] attributes his [Apollonius] theumaturgic feats not to the tricks of wizardry, but to a divine and mysterious wisdom; and he believes they were truly what he supposes them to have been, though he advances no proof of his contention. Listen then to his very words: 'In their anxiety to exalt Jesus, they run up and down printing of how he made the blind to see and worked certain other miracles of the kind.' Then after an interval he adds as follows: 'Let us note how much better and more sensible is the view which we take of such matters, and explain the conception which we entertain of men gifted with remarkable powers.' And thereupon after passing headlessly by Aristeas, continues thus: 'But in the time of our own ancestors, during the reign of Nero, there flourished Apollonius of Tyana who from mere boyhood when he became the priest of Aegae of Cicilia, of Ascalepius, the lover of mankind, worked any number of miracles, of which I will omit the greater number and only mention a few.'

"Then he begins at the beginning and enumerates the wonders worked by Apollonius, after which he continues in the following words: 'What then is my reason for mentioning these facts? It is in order that you may be able to contrast our own accurate and well-established judgment on each point with the easy credulity of the Christians. For whereas we reckon him who wrought such feats not a god, but only a man pleasing to the gods, they on the strength of a few miracles proclaim their Jesus a god.'

"To this he adds after a little more the following remark: 'And this point is also worth noticing, that whereas the tales of Jesus have been vamped up by Peter and Paul and a few others of the kind -- men who were liars and devoid of education and wizards -- the history of Apollonius was written by Maximus of Aegae, and by Damis the philosopher, who lived constantly with him, and by Philostratus of Athens, men of the highest education, who out of respect for the truth and their love of mankind, determined to give the publicity they deserved to the actions of a man at once noble and a friend of the gods."

These are the very words used by Hierocles in his treatise against us which he has entitled "Lover of Truth."*

(*Hierocles was inspired to write his book by Porphyry, who had written fifteen books against Christianity as well as many works in defense of Apollonius's neo- Pythagorean philosophy, including four books in defense of vegetarianism entitled "Four Books on Abstinence from Animal Food." Hierocles' work was written in 303 A.D., a year before Porphyry died.)

Hierocles was further answered by Lactantius; and it soon became necessary for every Catholic saint or doctor of the fourth and fifth centuries to have an opinion about Apollonius of Tyana. Eusebius admitted, however, that Apollonius was a great philosopher; and Lactantius and Arnobius, while not denying his miracles, attribute them to "magic." St. Jerome also regarded him as a magician. In a work written after the death of Philostratus by an unknown writer, which was formerly attributed to Justin Martyr, the miracles of Apollonius were further ascribed to magic.

St. Augustine, in arguing with the heathen, paid Apollonius a rather mild compliment by allowing that he was "purer than Jove." The learned Bishop Sidonius Apollonaris praised the Greek philosopher and translated his life into Latin. On the other hand, St. John Chrysostom branded the work of Philostratus as false and Apollonius as a "deceiver;" and his view gradually became the general one of Christian writers. The Church Father, Isidorus of Pelusium, who died in 450 A.D. bluntly denied that there was any truth in the assertion that Apollonius "consecrated many spots in the world for the safety of the inhabitants."

Among the ancient writers who make mention of Apollonius is Origen, who refers to the memoirs of Maeragenes; who speaks of him as a philosopher and magician. Later, Ammianus Marcellinus, the last subject of Rome who composed a profane history in the Latin language, and the friend of Julian the Philosopher, Emperor, refers to Apollonius as "that most renowned philosopher." and thought that, "like Pythagoras and Socrates, he was a privileged mortal who lived assisted by a familiar genius." A few years later, Eunapius, the pupil of Chrysanius, one of the teachers of Julian, writing in the last years of the fourth century says that, "Apollonius was more than a philosopher; he was a middle term, as it were, between gods and men."

Eunapius states furthermore that Apollonius was not only an adherent of the Pythagorean philosophy, but "he fully exemplified the more divine and practical side of it." He believes that Philostratus should have called his biography "The Sojourning of a God Among Men."

Even in the sixth century, after the downfall of philosophy with the rise of the Church, we find Cassiodorus, who spent the last years of his life in a monastery, speaking of Apollonius as the "renowned philosopher." In the eighth century, among the Byzantine writers, we find the monk, George Syncellus, referring to him as "the most remarkable of all the illustrious people who appeared under the Roman Empire." At about the same time, Tzetzos, a critic and grammarian, called Apollonius "all-wise and fore-knower of all things."

Towards the end of the middle ages, the cult of Apollonius still survived in the east, though forgotten in the west, as indicated by the Statement of Nicetus concerning the melting-down of certain bronze doors at Byzantium, which were said to have been inscribed with the "Book of Rites," one of the lost works of Apollonius. This was done to put an end to non-christian beliefs and usages which had gathered around them.

In the eleventh century, opinion [regarding Apollonius of Tyana] was divided; and while on the other hand, we find the monk Xiphillinus, in a note to his abridgement of the history of Dion Cassius, calls Apollonius "a clever juggler and magician," Cidrenus in the same century bestows on Apollonius the not uncomplimentary title of "an adept with efficacy of his power over the elements" in Byzantium.

Even as late as 1832, Bauer attempted to show that not only were there resemblances between the "Life of Apollonius of Tyana" and the Gospels, but that Philostratus deliberately modeled his hero on the type set forth by the Evangelists. He was followed in this view by Zeller, the celebrated Greek historian.

Typical of latter nineteenth century views on the subject is that of Cardinal Newman, a Catholic apologist, who, admitting the identity of

Apollonius and the Gospel messiah, considers the former an imitation of the latter, in spite of the fact that he preceded him by three centuries (For the Jesus of the Gospels was evidently born in the year 325 A.D., at the Council of Nicea, rather than when the star appeared over Bethlehem).

To support his view, Newman mentions certain typical examples, such as Apollonius's bringing to life a dead girl in Rome, which he considers as "an attempt, and an elaborate, pretentious attempt, to outdo certain narratives in the Gospels (Mark v. 29, Luke vii. John xi: 41-43, Acts iii: 4-6). This incident, is described by Philostratus.

Presenting further evidence that Philostratus's biography of Apollonius is in many ways a replica of the life of Jesus, Cardinal Newman writes: The favour in which Apollonius from a child was held by gods and men; his conversations when a youth in the Temple of Aesculapius; his determination, in spite of danger to go up to Rome; the cowardice of his disciples in deserting him; the charge brought against him of disaffection to Caesar; the Minister's acknowledging, on his private examination, that he was more than man; the ignominious treatment of him by Domitian on his second appearance at Rome; his imprisonment with criminals; his vanishing from Court and sudden reappearance to his mourning disciples at Puteoli--these, with other particulars of a similar cast, evidence a history modelled after the narrative of the Evangelists. Expressions, moreover, and descriptions occur, clearly imitated "from the sacred volume."

Reville, another Catholic apologist, thinks as does Newman that "the biography of Apollonius is in great measure an imitation of the Gospel narrative."* (*Reville bases his argument on the similarity of the characters of Apollonius and Pythagoras (which is natural in view of Apollonius following Pythagoras as his example); and he seeks to prove that Apollonius, rather than Jesus, is a fictitious creation, rather than an historical character. Reville writes: "It is hard to say whether the Pythagoras of the Alexandrians is not an Apollonius of an earlier date by some centuries, or whether the Apollonius of Julia Domna, besides his resemblance to Christ, is not a Pythagoras endowed with a second youth. The real truth of the matter will probably be found to lie between the two suggestions."

Godfrey Higgins considers Christ as an imitation of Pythagoras, who likewise started life immaculately and was killed by his enemies while seeking to serve mankind. The truth is that both Pythagoras and Apollonius were historical while Jesus is mythical.) This would imply that Philostratus's "Apollonius" had no real existence and was modeled on the life of Jesus.

In refutation of that claim, that Apollonius had no historical existence and is an imitation of Jesus, is the existence of a "Lease from the Estate of Apollonius," which is among the Zenon papyri acquired by Columbia University in 1926. It is a Greek manuscript written on parchment which refers to a gift of cultivated land bestowed by King Ptolemy, son of Ptolemy Soter, to Apollonius of Tyana; which was signed by Damis. The land produced barley and wheat, which yielded its owners a regular income.

The lease was a legal document which stipulated the revenue that Apollonius was to receive from the crops which the land produced, and to it the names of a number of witness were affixed. In view of such clear evidence of the historical existence of Apollonius, in sharp contract with the lack of such evidence concerning the Christian Son of God, the question as to whether Apollonius or Jesus - in the historical original of which the other is an imitation - finds the ready solution in the mind of every unbiased person.

Apollonius spoke in parables just as Jesus did. Concerning this point, Roberts, in his "Antiquity Unveiled," writes: "If the identity of style and sentiment is possible then the learned Apollonius was the original author of the teachings attributed to Jesus Christ; an identity that all the altering, eliminating and interpolating by the Christian hierarchy have not been able to destroy or even imperfectly conceal."

This similarity in the expressions of the two men made Cudworth, a Christian apologist, in his "Intellectual System," write: "It is highly improbable, if not unquestionable, that Apollonius of Tyana shortly after the publication of the gospel to the world, was a person made choice of by the policy and assisted by the powers of the kingdom of darkness, for doing something extraordinary, merely out of design to derogate from the miracles of our Saviour Jesus Christ, and to enable paganism the better to bear up against the attacks of Christianity."

Huet another apologist says further on the same subject, "He (Philostratus) aimed and thinks it to have been his principal design to obstruct the progress of the Christian religion by drawing the character of a man of great knowledge, sanctity and miraculous power. Therefore he forced Apollonius after the example of Christ and accommodated many things in the history of our Lord to Apollonius.

Thus the learned and pious Christian, Huet, was forced to admit the common identity of Apollonius and Jesus -- the first described by Philostratus according to the memoirs of Damis, written in the first century, and the other described by no one knows whom or when, but certainly not until several centuries later.*

(*Commenting on the opinion of Huet, and confirming his identification of Apollonius and Jesus, Parker, Archdeacon of Canterbury, in 1681, remarked: "I know that Huet is of the opinion, that all the substantial miracles (of Apollonius) are stolen out of the Acts of the Apostles, and for the most part, in the words and phrases of St. Luke. And this he had endeavored to make good by a great variety of parallel instances and thinks it a manifest discovery both of the vanity of Philostratus and the imposture of Apollonius, where he is only adorned with borrowed feathers but a great accession to the credit of our Saviour that when his enemies would form the idea of a divine man, they were forced to steal his best feathers from his picture. So that, he says, it was no wonder that Hierocles should so confidently compare the miracles of Apollonius to those of Jesus when those of Jesus were with so little disguise clapped upon Apollonius.")

As Christian writers have been forced to admit the identity of the respective narratives, concerning Apollonius and Jesus, the only question to be settled is, who was the original author of the so-called Christian teachings? There is sufficient evidence available to prove that Apollonius of Tyana was that author, and NOT Jesus of Nazareth nor Paul of Tarsus, as is wrongly claimed by Christian writers.

Now, there was another important reason for the suppression of Philostratus's book, besides the fact that it presented a dangerous rival to the Christian messiah. This was the fact that, though based on the notes of a contemporary of Jesus, and describing his travels from one end of the then known world to the other, throughout the work there is not a single mention of the existence of Jesus or Christianity, indicating that neither Damis, who wrote the original notes in the early part of the first century, or Philostratus, who compiled the notes two centuries later, were aware that either existed. Philostratus's biography was written about a century prior to the formation of the Church at the beginning of the fourth century, prior to the formation of the church (325 A.D.) and Catholics have taken special pains to destroy all books written at this time, lest the fact become known that none of them make mention of Jesus or of Christianity.

It was to destroy such books that the Alexandrian and other ancient libraries were burnt following the formation of the Church at the beginning of the fourth century prior to which Christianity (as we know and understand it) did not exist and Jesus was unknown.

The argument that there is almost complete silence in Philostratus's biography concerning the existence of Jesus and his disciples has been the one most frequently advanced by Catholics to each other, in order that there be maintained great vigilance in the suppression of this book. In such discussions, this was what was said: "There is most complete silence as regards to Jesus and his disciples. They are never mentioned; the existence of the Christian Church is ignored; and yet the book contains attacks on all kinds of religious and moral errors; hence, it is argued, any similarity which may exist between the life of Christ and that of the pagan reformer is either accidental, or formed." On this subject, Tredwell remarks that Christian writers "declare that Philostratus wrote up a character in imitation of Christ, and in opposition to the Christian religion, when the best evidence in the world exists (his entire silence) that he never heard of Christ or Christians. However, if Philostratus did create a character in imitation of Christ, how much more worthy of our imitation in practice and precept is the counterfeit!"

Had there been such persons living as Jesus Christ, his apostles and their Christian followers during the time that Apollonius lived and labored throughout the then civilized world, Damis, who accompanied him during much of that time, and who recorded every thing worthy of special note, would have made some mention of such people, either favorably on unfavorably. That he did not do so is, of itself, sufficient proof that neither Jesus Christ, his apostles nor the Christian religion had any existence either before or during that period, which was the only time in which they could have lived, if they really did.

Dr. Lardner, in his "Credibility of the Gospel Story," therefore writes:

"It is manifest, therefore, that Philostratus compared Apollonius and Pythagoras; but I do not see that he endeavored to make him a rival of Jesus Christ. Philostratus had never once mentioned our Saviour, or the Christians, his followers; neither in this long work, nor in the 'Lives of the Sophists;' if this be his as some learned men of the best judgment suppose, is there any hint that Apollonius anywhere in his wide travels, met with any followers of Jesus? There is not so much as an obscure or general description of any men met with by him, whom any can suspect to be Christians of any denomination, either Catholics or heretics. Whereas I think if Philostratus had written with a mind adverse to Jesus, he would have laid hold of some occasion to describe and disparage his followers, as enemies of the gods, and condemners of the mysteries and different from all other men."

Nevertheless it was this very absence of mention of Jesus and the Christians in Philostratus's book which was considered by the Catholic Church as sufficient reason to prohibit its publication for over a thousand years, lest it be suspected that no Christians existed at the time when the book was written and that Jesus never lived.

Dr. Lardner observes that just as there was no mention of Jesus or Christianity by Philostratus, so we find a similar silence about Apollonius in the works of early Christian writers, though they mention philosophers of much less renown, as Justin, Tatian, Clement of Alexandria, Tertullian, etc. Of all these we have some remains; they lived in the first two centuries and the beginning of the third. This silence on the part of these authors regarding Apollonius can be accounted for on the basis of only one theory - that it was necessary to utterly ignore Apollonius and his philosophical and religious teachings in order that the Christian religion might gain a foothold and usurp the field he had grandly occupied.

Besides, the fragmentary remains of the works of the first three centuries that have reached us, have had to pass through the hands of Eusebius, Pope Sylvester I, and their coadjutors and successors, who, from the beginning of the fourth century downward to the time when the art of printing ended it, were so assiduously engaged in interpolating, mutilating and destroying every trace of evidence within their reach that showed the real origin and nature of the Christian religion and its true founder. It should have struck the attention of Dr. Lardner, with vastly greater force, that just as in Philostratus's lengthy biography of Apollonius there is no mention of Jesus, so in the entire New Testament there is not a single mention of Apollonius, if we except in a few verses of lst Corinthians, where it says, "for while one saith, I am of Apollos, are ye not carnal? Who, then, is Paul, and who Apollos, but ministers by whom ye believed, even as the Lord gave to every man? I have planted, Apollos watered; but God gave the increase." [First Corinthians, Chapter 3, Verses 3-6; King James Version].

In a very ancient manuscript of this Epistle, found in a monastery in France by a Huegenot soldier, called the CODEX BEZAE, the name is spelled not Apollos but APOLLONIUS. As has already been indicated, the Encyclopedia Britannica admits that the name, Apollos, as it appears in the Pauline Epistles, is an abbreviation of Apollonius.**

**But even this positive clue to the identity of Apollonius with the St. Paul of the Christians was attempted to be obliterated by substituting "Apollos" for Apollonius, as it originally stood. This studied avoidance of all mention of Apollonius in the Christian Scriptures is positive proof that his recognition, in any way, by the authors of Christianity, would be fatal to their scheme of deception and fraud. We Wonder they had not the cunning to obliterate that one reference to the preaching and teaching of Apollonius, and the admission that his teaching was in perfect accord with the teachings attributed to St. Paul.

It is an old saying that liars should have good memories. This was never more apparent than in the oversight of not eliminating that telltale confession from the lst Epistle to the Corinthians. [King James Version]. There it stands and there it will stand, thanks to the art of printing to confound those Christian enemies of truth and make clear the fraud they are upholding.

Reversing the true state of affairs, involving as it did the replacement of Apollonius by Jesus in the beginning of the fourth century A.D., Dr. Johannese Hempel writes: "In the fourth century we observe the replacement by the heathens of Jesus by a man who was put in his place. First Celsus and Porphyry, and later Hierocles put Apollonius in place of Christ and opposed the new religion.

Reversing the true state of affairs, involving as it did the replacement of Apollonius by Jesus in the beginning of the fourth century A.D., Dr. Johannese Hempel writes: "In the fourth century we observe the replacement by the heathens of Jesus by a man who was put in his place. First Celsus and Porphyry, and later Hierocles put Apollonius in place of Christ and opposed the NEW religion."

(**In the Eleventh Edition of the Encyclopedia Britannica under the heading of Apollos, we read: APOLLOS (contracted from Apollonius) - an Alexandrian Jew who after Paul's visit to Corinth worked there in a similar way (Italics ours). He was with Paul at a later date in Ephesus. In Cor. 1. 10-12 we read of four parties in the Corinthian church, of which two attached themselves to Paul and Apollos respectively, using their names, though the 'division' could hardly be due to conflicting doctrines. From Acts xviii. 24-288 we learn that he spoke and taught with power and success., He may have captivated his hearers by teaching "wisdom" as P.W. Schmiedel suggests, in the allegorical style of Philo, and he was evidently a man of unusual magnetic force...Since Apollos was a Christian and 'taught exactly' he could hardly have been acquainted only with John's baptism or have required to be taught christianity more thoroughly by Aquila and Priscilla. Martin Luther regarded Apollos [=Apollonius] as the author of the Epistle to the Hebrews and many scholars since have shared his view.")

Concerning the identity of Apollonius and Paul ["Pol", an abbreviation of Apollonius), not only were they both in Tarsus at the same time as boys, but, as Newman points out, Apollonius was at Ephesus and Rome at EXACTLY the same time that Paul was (yet, strangely, Apollonius's biographer makes no mention of him, though Paul's biographer speaks of "Apollos" having been at Ephesus with him). Also it is significant that "Paul" is a fictitious name. There is more reason to identify the character of Apollonius with Paul than "Saul," who led a dissipated life, while Apollonius - even in youth, lived chastely.

Concerning the identity of Apollonius, with Paul, Reville writes: "Apollonius is not only like Jesus Christ, but he combines in his own person many of the characteristics of the Apostles. Like Paul he travels up and down the world from east to west, and like him, too, he is the victim of Nero's jealousy. Like John, according to a tradition which prevailed even in his time, he is persecuted by Domitian." And there is reason to believe that he was also the author of the Apocalypse (St. John the Revelator).

The replacement of the vegetarian and pacifistic doctrine of Apollonius, who taught harmlessness to all living beings, animal as well as human (as was previously taught by gotama Buddha), by the non-vegetarian and non-pacifistic religion of Jesus and his bride, the Church Militant, has plunged the world into centuries of unceasing wars and bloodshed, which have continued to increase with the growth of Christianity. On this point, Tredwell writes; "Think not that I come to send peace on earth," said Jesus. "I come not to send peace but a sword....

Never did a man utter words so brimful of truth -- melancholy as it is. Never was a prediction whose disastrous fulfillment has unfortunately lasted without intermission from time time of its promulgation to the present. From the very establishment of the religion of Jesus, the sword has remained unsheathed in its service, and more victims have been sacrificed to its manes than to all other causes combined. Lest he should be misunuderstood concerning his mission Jesus reiterates that he came to send fire on earth, and strife to make divided households, fathers against sons, mothers against daughters, and that under the new regime, "a man's foes shall be those of his own household! Bolingbroke says, "The scene of Christianity has always been a scene of dissension, of hatred, of persecution and of blood." Erasmus said the church was born in blood; grew in blood; succeeded in blood, and will end in blood."

Tredwell pointed out that Christianity forced its way forward by mass executions and at the point of the sword. It was in this way that the "Church Militant" was born and was enabled to develop as a world power. Born in bloodshed (the brutal murder of Hypatia by Christian "monks" soon after the Council of Nicea, by order of Cyril, Bishop of Alexandria, who was subsequently "sainted," and the ensuing massacres of the Manicheans), it grew by bloodshed (the deaths of tens of millions of true followers of Christ, who refused to accept the false hypocritical teachings of the church, over three million women having been put to death in Europe only a few centuries ago as witches), it shall die in bloodshed (the aftermath of the recent world carnage which is fruit of sixteen centuries of false Christian teachings of peace, carried on with an olive branch in one hand and a sword in the other).

All this resulted from the fraudulent replacement of the original religion of Apollonius by the "new" religion of the Church of Rome which took place at the Council of Nicea in the year 325 B.C.*

(*The word "new" here is significant. It clearly indicates that at the beginning of the fourth century, Christianity, as created by the Council of Nicea, was indeed a new religion, and was preceded by the religion established by Apollonius three centuries previously, which may be more properly called Essenism, a form of Neo-Pythagoreanism in character, the new doctrines which Apollonius brought from India and introduced among the Essenes, which gave rise to the new sect known as the NAZARENES or THERAPEUTS, whose doctrines were essentially Buddhist in nature.)

Since this date humanity has been led astray. It is the purpose of this book to correct this historic error and to bring humanity back to the truth, so that, purged by the recent suffering, mankind once more will return to the true scientific path of natural, healthful and humane living taught by the great Pythagorean philosopher, Apollonius of Tyana, nearly two thousand years ago.

Part 4   *Events in the life of Apollonius of Tyana*

When the three magi of Chaldea were approaching Bethlehem, according to legend on the night when the famous star was supposed to have appeared on the eastern horizon, a child was born in the little town of Tyana, in Cappadocia, who was destined to alter the course of human history for two thousand years -- even though, as the Delphic Oracle predicted, after his passing, his name was calumniated, and a fictitious substitute put in his place.

The country people said that he was the son of Zeus; others called him a son of Apollo; while still others considered him as an incarnation of Proteus, the God of Wisdom, who, prior to his birth, appeared to his mother and told her that she would bear a child who would be an incarnation of himself.

Apollonius was born in the year 4 B.C., the acknowledged year of the birth of Christ. His birth, like his conception, was miraculous. Just before his nativity, his mother was walking in a meadow, where she lay down on the grass and went to sleep. Some wild swans, at the end of a long flight approached her and by their cries and the beating of their wings, awakened her so suddenly that her child was born before its time. The swans, apparently, had foreseen and marked by their presence the fact that on that day was to be born a being whose soul would be as white as their own plumage and who, like them, would be a glorious wanderer.

Apollonius was born with three gifts, the gift of intelligence, the gift of beauty and the gift of wealth. His father was one of the richest men of the province, so that his childhood was spent in luxury. The renown of his intelligence and beauty grew so great that the phrase, "Whither goest thou? To see the stripling?" became proverbial in Cappadocia.

When he was fourteen years of age, his father sent him to Tarsus to complete his education, which was previously conducted at home by private tutors. Tarsus was a town of pleasure as well as study and life there was soft and luxurious for a rich young man. On the banks of the Cydnus, along avenues bordered by orange trees, students of philosophy gathered to discuss the theories of Pythagoras and Plato with young women in colored tunics slashed to the hip, wearing Egyptian high triangular combs in their hair. The climate was hot, morals free and love easy, but the youthful Apollonius was not carried away, manifesting at this young age the same inviolate chastity which he continued to preserve throughout his long life of over a century, in spite of the fact that he was one of the handsomest men of his age.

As early as his fourteenth year, Apollonius recognized the existence of two divergent paths, one leading to a life of pleasure and love, and the other to philosophy and wisdom; and he chose the latter.*

(*Shirley says that Apollonius "chose the path of sanctity at a time of life when others chose the primrose path of dalliance...The world holds no record of a long life lived more nobly, of a more undaunted courage in confronting the tyrant, of a more unflinching tenacity of purpose, of a more single-minded devotion to a high ideal." While himself living an ascetic life, Apollonius sought to make Venus the goddess of pure love, free from carnal lust, rather than to destroy her statue altogether, as the later Christians did.)

He then decided to lead the Pythagorean life. When his teacher of Pythagorean philosophy, Euxenes, asked him how he would begin his new mode of life, he replied, "As doctors purge their patients." "Hence," says Mead, in his biography, "he refused to touch anything that had animal life in it, on the ground that it densified the mind and rendered it impure. He considered that the only pure form of food was what the earth produced -- fruits and vegetables.* He also abstained from wine, for though it was made from fruit, it rendered turbid the ether in the soul, and destroyed the composure of the mind."

(*Concerning Apollonius as a vegetarian, Phillimore, in his "In Honor of Apollonius of Tyana," writes: "A man called Apollonius was born at Tyana at some date known, probably in the reign of Tiberius. The persecutions which made it dangerous for Seneca at Rome to continue his experiment in vegetarianism did not extend to Cilicia, and Apollonius addicted himself to Neo-Pythagoreanism (vegetarianism.) From the ordinary humanistic training of a sophist, he seems to have passed into the ascetic discipline of a sect which, originally Oriental, and afterwards reaching its highest success among the decadent colonial aristocracies of South Italy, was now again coming into vogue as the Roman empire began to orientalize. Indian theosophy, a natural science chiefly drawn from Stoic authorities, antiquarian ritualism in certain Greek cults, a great copiousness of moral sentiment, the asceticism which usually appear at the times when the white corpuscles predominate in the body politic of any civilization -- vegetarianism, teetotalism, etc., -- such appear to have been the main ingredients in Apollonius's religion.")

Finding the morals of Tarsus distasteful, Apollonius resolved to take up quarters at Aegae, which possessed a temple of Aesculapius, the priests of which were philosophers of the Pythagorean school. So famous were they for their power as healers that people came to their temple from all over Greece, from Syria and even from Alexandria to consult them. The priests of this healing temple of Aegae cured disease by vegetarian diet, hydrotherapy, fasting and magnetic healing ("laying on of hands," which art, Apollonius acquired from them). They were heirs of an ancient oral therapeutic tradition which came from the Orphic mysteries, the secret of which was jealously guarded by the disciple who received it. By these priests, Apollonius was initiated; and it was not long before he excelled his masters.

Concerning Apollonius's life in the temple of Aegae, Stobart writes: "Marvelous cures are attributed to Apollonius, for like his great master, Pythagoras, he considered healing the most important of the divine arts; and, in addition, under his guidance, the temple became also a centre for philosophy and for the science of religion. His aim was to purify the temple worship and to reform the ancient Greek religion from within, by revising, along Pythagorean lines, the understanding of the spiritual truths which were at the base of the esoteric mysteries."*

(*The school of Pythagoras formed at that time a secret order which had several stages of initiation, the members of which recognized each other by certain signs and symbols, in order that the doctrine remain unintelligible to the profane. Music, geometry and astronomy were studied, but not as they are now but rather as discipline to prepare the mind for the awakening of super-sensory spiritual facilities of perception. The aim of the Pythagorean teaching was physical, mental and spiritual regeneration, which Pythagoras founded on a vegetarian diet and continence. The members of the Pythagorean Order so carefully guarded their secret doctrines that the Pythagorean Timycha cut out her tongue rather than reveal to Dionysus the Elder the reason for the prohibition of beans in the rules of the community.)

Apollonius took up his residence in the temple of Aesculapius at Aegae in the company of the priests, manifesting an amazing eagerness to acquire their secret knowledge, and had an astonishing gift for healing and clairvoyance. And, following Pythagorean custom, he let his hair grow long, abstained from the flesh of animals and from wine; walked barefooted or with bark sandals, and clad only in white linen garments, giving up all that was made from leather, wool or any other animal material.

At this time being then sixteen years of age, he resolved to forever abstain from marriage and sexual relations, which resolution he kept unbroken during his long lifetime of over a century, thus surpassing Pythagoras, Socrates, Buddha and Confucius, for while they married, Apollonius preserved a degree of virginity known only to vestal virgins and Pythian priestesses. This immaculate chastity Apollonius attributed to his very careful Pythagorean low-protein vegetarian diet and his avoidance of alcohol and other excitants, according to the teaching of Pythagoras, who prohibited even vegetable proteins such as beans, for this reason.

Concerning the life of Apollonius at this age, W. B. Wallace writes:

"Hence forth Apollonius adjured all the pleasures of sense. A vegetarian and a total abstainer in the modern meaning of the latter term, the devoted monk of philosophy adopted and practiced more rigidly than any hermit of the Thebaid, the triple rule of poverty, chastity and obedience."* This native of a warm and luxuriant clime, whose people were wholly given to indolent gossip and sybaritic enjoyments of all kinds, was clad in a simple robe of white byssus, after the fashion of Empedocles, whom he so much resembled in many ways, slept upon the ground, went bare-footed like Socrates, and -- hardest trial of all to a talkative Asiatic Greek -- observed the Pythagorean silence for five years."*

(*Concerning the young Apollonius's resolution to lead a Pythagorean life, his biographer, Philostratus, writes: "Naught would he wear that came from a dead beast, nor touch a morsel of a thing that once had life, nor offer it in sacrifice; nor for him to stain with blood the altars; but honey-cakes and incense, and the service of his song went upward from the man unto the Gods [higher-dimensional spiritual intelligences] for well he knew that they would take such gifts far rather than the oxen in their hundreds with the knife. For, he in sooth, held converse with the Gods and learned from them how they were pleased with men and how displeased, and thence as well he drew his nature-lore. As for the rest, he said, they guessed at the divine, and held opinions on the Gods which proved each other false; but unto him Apollo's self did come, confessed without disguise, and there did come as well, though unconfessed, Athena and the Muses, and other Gods [spiritual rulers or Lords of inner spiritual planes, viz. astral, mental, and causal planes] whose forms and names mankind did not yet know."

"Thus passed the 'lehr-jare' of Apollonius, and thus in the very heydey of his youth was the flesh subdued to the spirit. It is certain that none but a lofty soul, favoured with a vision of the Supreme rarely vouchsafed to man, could have voluntarily embraced a life of hardness such as this. And yet the man never allowed asceticism to degenerate into misanthropy. A perennial fount of joy seemed to bubble within his soul. He had a smiling countenance and a sparkling eye; in mien and aspect he was striking, dignified, godlike; his nature was kindly and sympathetic; he liked the society of his fellows and the encounter of mind and mind; he was a past master in the art of repartee and a cunning fabricator of 'bon-mots', of which Philostratus has preserved several examples."

At Aegae, Apollonius took up the study of Pythagorean philosophy, which was the system that appealed to him most, under a teacher named Euxenes; who, however, proved disappointing, since he repeated parrot-like, the doctrines of Pythagoras without putting them into practice in his own life, for he was a materialist at heart. So Apollonius, in disillusionment, left him; however rewarding his teacher by buying for him a villa surrounded by a garden outside Aegae, and giving him the money required for his servants, his suppers and his poor friends.

Apollonius then imposed on himself a five years' silence, which was considered necessary in order to achieve final Pythagorean initiation. By that time he had become famous, making many prophecies that came true; and while he was in the midst of this period of silence, he quelled a rebellion by his presence alone, without speaking a word. This tumult was caused by a famine at Aspendus in Pamphylia, where the people were going to burn the prefect, though he had taken refuge by a statue of the Emperor. (And at that time, which was the reign of Tiberius, the Emperor's statues were more terrible and more inviolable than those of the Olympian Zeus.) The prefect, on being questioned by signs, protested his innocence, and accused certain powerful citizens, who were refusing to sell corn and keeping it back to export at a profit. To them Apollonius addressed a note threatening "explusion from Earth, who is the mother of all, for she is just, but whom they, being unjust, have made the mother of themselves alone." In fear of this threat they yielded and filled the market-place with corn.

Part 5   Apollonius' Visit to the Brahman Sages of the Himalayas

Apollonius's attention was then drawn to India, the fountain-head of Wisdom. Five centuries previously, Pythagoras had brought some of the Himalayan wisdom to Greece. But its memory had almost vanished. The world was in need of a new emissary of the eastern masters. Apollonius believed that he was called to perform such a mission; and so he set out, accompanied only by his friend and disciple, Damis, on the long and perilous trip to the Himalayas, following the same route formerly traversed by Pythagoras when he traveled to India on a similar mission five hundred years before.

This was revealed to Apollonius at a half-abandoned temple of Daphnaean Apollo some distance from Antioch, where a peasant-priest brought him the temple treasure, which had been preserved by tradition, handed down from father to son. This consisted of some sheets of copper on which were figures and diagrams. The priest had zealously preserved them till that moment; awaiting the arrival of the man worthy to receive this gift.

While engaged in his early morning devotions in the light of the rising sun, the priest gave Apollonius the copper sheets, which, as a Pythagorean, he was able to decipher as a record of his Master's journey to India, including the deserts and high mountains to be crossed before he reached the river in which elephants disport themselves. He also saw before him a description of the exact spot which he had to reach (in trans-Himalayan Tibet), and of the monastery among the thousands of monasteries in the Far East where, five centuries previously, Pythagoras had studied at the feet of the same Masters who were soon to become his teachers.

For Apollonius was to become their new western emissary, as Pythagoras had been five centuries previously.*

(*Apollonius was to be the last western emissary of the Masters of the Far East for many centuries. After him the door was shut. The Neo-Pythagorean, Plotinus, two centuries later, tried in vain to follow in his steps and reach India together with the armies of the Emperor Gordianus, but was compelled to turn back. It was not until a few centuries ago that the Masters found their next great emissary in Conte St. Germain (Francis Bacon), who, like Apollonius, retired to the Himalayas after his passing from the eyes of the world.)

Reaching the little town of Mespila, which had once been Ninevah, Apollonius met his future traveling companion and disciple, Damis, who immediately was attached to him and remained with him as his follower throughout his life. Apollonius accepted him as his guide to take him to Babylon, since Damis said he knew the way there perfectly, and boasted, too, of knowing the languages spoken in the countries through which they would have to pass: To this Apollonius smiled and replied that he himself knew all languages spoken by men and understood their silence as well.

(Damis was later to realize that he also possessed knowledge of the language of birds, and could read the great characters, against the blue of the sky, formed by the trajectory of their flight. It is claimed that it was from the Arabian philosophers that Apollonius learned to understand the speech of animals.)

Apollonius's chief public work was that of religious reform, involving the abolition of animal sacrifices, which he replaced by bloodless offerings that involved the death of no living being. The following incident is cited concerning his teachings of kindness to animals, which constituted the basis of his opposition to animal sacrifices and his advocacy of vegetarianism.

When he reached Babylon, after refusing to do obeisance to the golden image of the king, the latter, who knew him already by repute, called him and, about to sacrifice a white horse to the sun, he asked Apollonius to accompany him. Apollonius refused, replying, "You, O King, sacrifice in your own manner, and give me leave to sacrifice in mine." Then, having thrown frankincense on the flame, and uttered a prayer to the god, he departed, so as to have no share in an offering of blood. When the king invited him to join him in hunting the animals of his park, he expressed disapproval of the pleasure taken in hunting and killing of wild animals kept for sport.

After they had spent some time with the magi of Babylon and conversed with them, the two travelers, Apollonius and Damis, climbed mountains whose summits were veiled in the clouds. Unaffected by the gradual unfolding of their snowy immensities, Apollonius said "When the soul is without blemish it can rise far above the highest mountains." (into the higher spiritual planes). They crossed the Indus and came across kings clothed in white who despised ostentation. One evening, on a lonely river bank, they came on a brass stele inscribed with the words; "Here Alexander halted."

Coming into the land of elephants, (India), nomads offered Apollonius date wine, which he refused, though he did not forbid Damis to take it, just as he did not refuse him to eat flesh, not wishing to impose his will on his disciple; however, he himself abstained from both.

Coming to the court of Phroates, King of Taxila, Apollonius was hospitably received by this vegetarian emperor who led a Pythagorean life except for his mild use of wine. When he tried to argue with Apollonius concerning the benefits of the moderate use of wine, saying that it promotes restful sleep, Apollonius, defended his water-drinking, saying it preserves the soul untroubled and makes true divination (clairvoyance) through dreams possible, with which wine interferes.

Following the course of the Ganges, they climbed more hills and mountains (the Himalayas), and when they were eighteen days' march from the Ganges, they saw in the middle of a plateau (Tibet) high in the mountains, the home of the wise men, which had the same elevation as the Acropolis at Athens. A strange fog hovered over the place, and on the rocks surrounding it were the imprints of men who appeared to have fallen in an attempt to scale the heights, for an almost perpendicular ascent was necessary at this point.

Then a young Indian approached the travelers, and coming over to Apollonius, speaking in perfect Greek, he told him to halt and follow him upwards, saying the Masters were expecting their arrival and had commanded him to go to receive the visitors. Apollonius and Damis were then led by their guide towards the community of Brahman sages dwelling on the Himalayan heights, whose chief was IARCHUS, a great Buddhist religious reformer. Philostratus described these sages as "Brahmans who dwell on the earth, and yet are not on the earth; in places fortified, and yet without walls; and who possess nothing and yet all things.*

(*From de Beauvoir Preiaulaux, in his "The Indian Travels of Apollonius of Tyana," we gather the following facts about these Brahmans , whom he describes as a race superior to the rest of mankind. He writes: "The Brahman's education began even in his mother's womb. During the period of gestation she was soothed by song and chants in praise of continence, which in proportion as they won her pleased attention, beneficially influenced her future offspring. After the child's birth, and as it grew in years, it was passed from one preceptor to another, until it was old enough to become an auditor of the philosophers. These lived frugally, abstained from animal food and women, and in a grove outside the city spent their days in earnest discourse, communicating their knowledge to all who chose to listen. But in their presence, the novice was not permitted to speak, or spit, under the penalty of one day's banishment from their society. At the age of thirty-seven, his student life ceased.

"The mountain Brahmans subsist on fruit and cow's curd with herbs. The others live on the fruit trees which are found in plenty near the river and which afford an almost constant succession of fresh fruits, and, should these fail, on the self-sown wild rice that grows there. To eat any other food, or even touch animal food, they held to be the height of impiety and uncleanliness. Each man has his own cabin, and lives as much as he can by himself, and spends the day and the greater part of the night in hymns and prayers to the gods....")

(According to Damis, the Brahmans used the earth as a couch, but first strewed it with choice grasses. They walked, too, in the air; Damis saw them. He saw too, the fire which they drew from the sun's rays, while they worshipped the solar orb. Among their other miraculous powers were the capacity to cover themselves with clouds at will, and to get what they wanted at a moment's notice [yogic practices which yield `siddhis' or supernatural powers -- utilizing undiscovered laws of nature]. Damis describes these marvelous men as being strict vegetarians, who lived exclusively on fruits and vegetables. They were attired in a sleeveless one-piece linen dress; wearing no material of animal origin. They wore their hair long, which custom they explained on the basis of the physiological and psychological benefits which they considered the hair to impart to the brain. Just as the skin absorbs and transmits solar energy to the body as a whole, so they believed that the hair performs a similar function in relation to the brain, for which reason they exposed their long hair to the sun as often as possible, hoping thus to absorb as much as possible of the ultraviolet solar rays so powerful at the high altitude where they dwelt.)

And so saying he told Apollonius who his father was, his mother, all that happened to him at Aegae, and how Damis joined him, and what they had said and done on the journey; and he related this so distinctly and fluently, that he might have been a companion of their route. Apollonius, greatly astonished, asked him how he knew all this.

"In this knowledge," he answered, "You are not wholly wanting, and where you are deficient, we will instruct you, for methink it not well to keep secret what is worthy of being known especially from you, Apollonius -- a man of most excellent memory. And memory, you must know, is of the gods the one we most honor.

"But how do you know my nature?" asked Apollonius.

"We," he answered, "see into the very soul, tracing out its qualities by a thousand signs. But as midday is at hand, let us to our devotions in which you also may, if you will take part."*

[*The Indian yogic science is not based on outer "sun" worship. The yogi meditates on the inner "sun" or inner spiritual light which can be seen by the "third eye" between and behind the two eyebrows, which reveals itself when the attention is held steadily fixed at this inner centre (ajna chakra) within the astral body. The outer sun, symbolic of the inner spiritual splendour within, is only an outer symbol of devotion to the inner spiritual light (Naad, Word or Logos)].

Apollonius then asked Iarchus what opinion the Brahmans held of themselves, and was told that they held themselves to be "gods" [advanced spiritual beings] because they were good men, who knew all things because they first knew themselves." Iarchus then told Apollonius his former lives, stating that in his [former] incarnation he was an Egyptian sailor.

The Brahmans then undressed and took a bath, after which they put garlands on their heads around their long hair, and proceeded to the temple, intent on their hymns. There (quoting Damis's account), standing round in a circle, with Iarchus as their leader, they beat the ground with their staves, till bellying like a wave, it sent them up into the air about two cubits; and they then sang a hymn, very like the paeon of Sophocles sung at Athens to Aesculapius. They then descended to earth."* (*According to Philostratus, the Brahmans levitate at will in the air "not for the sake of vain glory, but to be nearer their Sun God," to whom they pray.)

When Apollonius asked the Brahmans whether, since they knew everything, whether they knew themselves, they replied in Socratic fashion, We know everything just because we begin by knowing ourselves, for no one of us would be admitted to this philosophy unless he first knew himself." When Apollonius inquired of Iarchus whether the cosmos was composed of Four elements, the latter replied that it was made not of four but of five, the fifth being the ether. There is, said the Indian sage, "the ether, which we must regard as the stuff of which gods are made, for just as mortal creatures inhale the air, so do immortal and divine natures inhale the ether."

On an occasion when he was praising Apollonius for his devotion to mystic lore, Iarchus said, "My great friend Apollonius, those who take pleasure in divination [clairvoyance--a byproduct of the awakening of dormant latent spiritual powers in the average man] are rendered divine thereby and contribute to the salvation of mankind."

The word "salvation" embraced for Iarchus both spiritual and physical health, for he declared that among the many blessings which the art of divination conferred upon mankind, the gift of healing was the most important, and to this art of divination he emphatically attributed "the credit of discovering simples which healed the bites of venomous creatures, and in particular of using the virus itself as a cure for many diseases. For I do not think" he added, "that men without the forecasts of a prophetic wisdom, would ever have ventured to mingle with medicines that save life, those deadly of poisons."

Thus we see Iarchus instructing his student, Apollonius of Tyana, in the science of medicine, as he instructed him in astrology and other sciences. Reville, in his "Apollonius of Tyana, the Pagan Christ of the Third Century," writes as follows concerning the Brahmans: "They worshipped fire, which they boasted had been brought down directly from the.sun... With his own eyes, Damis saw these sages rise up into the air to the height of two cubits, without any extraneous support and without any trickery whatsoever. The wise men do not live in houses, and when it rains they summon a cloud and shelter under it. They wear their hair long, have white mitres on their heads, and are clothed in linen garments, woven from a peculiar kind of flax which is only lawful for themselves to gather. Their prodigious wisdom overwhelmed even Apollonius, who was not frequently astonished. They are in possession of absolute science; they know at once the past history of every one they see; they can answer all questions. When asked, "Who are you?" they answer, We are `god.' Why? Because we are virtuous." [See "The Life and Teachings of the Masters of the Far East" by Baird T. Spalding, in 5 volumes, for a detailed account of the advanced spiritual sciences practised by the Himalayan yogic adepts of India and Tibet].

The Brahmans were furnished with everything they needed as a spontaneous gift of the earth, partaking of fresh vegetables and fruits in season which were brought to them by their countrymen dwelling below them. During his repast with the Brahman sages and their king, Apollonius and Damis were amazed to observe that the food was brought to their tables by self-moving tripods, while automata served as cup-bearers; these mechanical robot waiters making the use of human servants unnecessary.*

[*Atlantean technology is known to be secretly stored in underground caverns beneath the Potala at Lhasa, and in the many other caves that network underneath the sedimentary structures of the Himalayan mountains. Here we a have a demonstration of some of the lost technology being displayed, two thousand years before our supposedly advanced technological age].

Apollonius observed his teacher, Iarchus, perform miracles identical with those purported to have been performed by the New Testament messiah, such as, driving evil spirits out of a woman who was possessed, curing a cripple, restoring sight to a blind man and restoring a man with paralyzed hands to health. He had a high degree of clairvoyance, could see at any distance, beheld both past and future, and could tell the past lives of those he met.

Reville notes that Apollonius studied astrology and the science of divination under Iarchus, for these sessions were secret and to them Damis was not admitted, nor would Apollonius reveal to him the esoteric knowledge then imparted to him by his Himalayan teacher. [Advanced astrology can reveal the dates and times of previous incarnations of an individual; it is an exact science when properly understood and applied. The popular version commonly available today is but an enfeebled version of the true astrology, which reveals the inner outworkings of the karmic wheel, which balances all causes with corresponding effects.]

During his stay among the Brahman sages, Apollonius was instructed by his Master in the basic doctrines of reformed Buddhism, of which movement Iarchus was the recognized leader, who had fled to his far-off Himalayan retreat to escape persecution by the established Brahman priesthood of India. Apollonius carried westward the Buddhist teachings which he received from Iarchus in the form of certain Buddhist gospels, otherwise known as the DIEGESIS or the ORIGINAL GOSPEL, which he translated and rewrote, adapting it to the language and psychology of his native land.

Among the ESSENES he found the first converts to this new doctrine, the gospel of Chrishna; and those who followed these teachings (the Essenian Therapeuts, who were otherwise known as NAZARENES) subsequently became known as the first Christians. On his departure Iarchus gave Apollonius Seven rings named after the seven planets, one of which was to be worn on one day of the week; these seven rings would, he said, impart health and long life. Before parting, Iarchus prophesied that Apollonius would, even during his life, attain the honors of a divinity.

Thus for several months Apollonius lived among men who were `gods' in human form, and from them he learned spiritual wisdom which he was destined to later bring back to the west as the basis of a new religion (Christianity) of which he was to be the founder. It was from Iarchus that he received the mission that was to send him wandering all his life among the temples of the Mediterranean countries, for the purpose of restoring the ancient mysteries to their former purity.

When he left his Brahman master, Apollonius had certain assurance that he would thereafter be in constant telepathic communication with him and receive his guidance and instruction wherever he may be--which later actually was the case.*

(*On this subject, Magre, speaking of the Inner Voice on which Apollonius always relied for guidance, writes: "We shall never know to what order the spirit-guide of Apollonius belonged; whether the being who advised him took on a form as chaste as himself and as beautiful as the statue of the gods which he liked to contemplate, or whether the voice came from a distant Master who wished to see his pupil carry out the mission with which he entrusted him.

"I shall continue to speak to you as though you were present," Apollonius had said as he left his Indian Masters.

"Was it their words that he heard at a distance? Did he by divine inspiration receive the influx of their wise thoughts? The man to whom he gave the name of Iarchus must have brought the consolation of distant support to the untiring traveler, the wandering mystic.")

Part 6   *Apollonius Leaves Iarchus and*
                  Returns to Greece

Thus Apollonius departed from his master and teacher. And is it not possible that just as the name of Apollonius, in the New Testament, was changed to that of Jesus, so Iarchus became his "Father," while the Brahmans dwelling on the heights of the Himalayas became "angels in heaven"? As a farewell gift, the Brahman sages, on the threshold of their valley of mediation, gave Apollonius and Damis camels on which to cross India westward to the Red Sea, where they continued their journey by water.

Apollonius returned to Greece from India to accomplish the same mission that Pythagoras had done before him, namely, to carry westward the Wisdom of the East, for which his predecessor won only persecution, ending in the burning of the Pythagorean meeting-house in which Pythagoras and his disciples were assembled.*

(*Indicating that on his departure from the Brahmans, Apollonius considered himself as their emissary to accomplish in Greece what their last student, Pythagoras, had done five centuries previously, Mrs. St. Clair Stoddard writes, "Thus he conceived it to be his mission to restore to the Greeks something of the ancient wisdom of Pythagoras. And at the conclusion of these travels he was indeed abundantly endowed with occult (spiritual) wisdom which powerfully enforced his own supernormal gifts and on returning to Greece he was regarded as a divine person."

That Apollonius considered himself as continuing the work that Pythagoras had initiated five centuries previously is indicated by his statement to the spirit of Achilles, in which he referred to Pythagoras as "my spiritual ancestor.")

On his way home, Apollonius sent the following letter to Iarchus:

"Iarchus and the other sages, from Apollonius, greetings: I came to you by land; with your aid I return by sea, and might have returned even by air -- such is the wisdom you have imparted to me."*

(* de Beauvoir Priaulaux, in his "The Indian Travels of Apollonius of Tyana," written in 1873, comments as follows on this statement: "Easy and pleasant as this mode of travel [air] is thought to be, Apollonius had recourse to it but once -- on that memorable occasion when about midday he disappeared before the tribunal of Domitian, and the same evening met Damis at Ciachaerchia.")

"Even among the Greeks I shall not forget these things, and shall still hold commerce with you -- or I have indeed vainly drunk of the cup of Tantalus. Farewell, ye best philosophers."

According to another translation, Apollonius's letter read as follows:

"I came to you by land and ye have given me the sea, rather, by sharing with me your wisdom, ye have given me power to travel through heaven. These things will I bring back to the mind of the Greeks, and I will hold converse with you as though ye were present, if it be that I have not drunk of the cup of Tantalus in vain."*

(*From Iarchus, his master, Apollonius received the "cup of Tantalus," symbolizing the wisdom which it was his mission to bring back to Greece as Pythagoras had done before him. Tantalus is fabled to have stolen the cup of nectar from the gods; this was the "amrita," the ocean of immortality and wisdom of the Hindus.)

Mead in his "Apollonius of Tyana," makes the following comment on this quotation: "It is evident from these cryptic sentences that the 'sea' and the 'cup of Tantalus' are identical with the 'wisdom' which had been imparted to Apollonius -- a wisdom which he was to bring back once more to the memory of the Greeks. He thus clearly states that he returned from India with a distinct mission and with the means to accomplish it, for not only had he drunk of the ocean of wisdom in that he has learnt the Brahma Vidya* from their lips, but he has also learnt how to converse with them though his body be in Greece and their bodies in India." [*Brahma Vidya: the knowledge of Brahman or God, the universal spiritual Consciousness which creates, sustains and permeates the entire cosmos].

Part 7   *Labors of Apollonius in Greece*

On returning to Greece, Apollonius traveled around from city to city, visiting the temples, where he restored the ancient mysteries by reeducating the priests. According to Mead, Apollonius's "one idea seems to have been to spread abroad among the religious brotherhoods and institutions of the Empire some portion of the Wisdom which he brought back from India."

His work was to unify diverse creeds by revealing their common origin and nature, and thus to promote the Brotherhood of Mankind. His first work was to abolish the barbarous custom of animal sacrifices and to replace this by offerings of frankincense and flowers. His object was to turn the minds of priests and laymen from the EXTERNAL FORMS of religion, from rituals and sacrifices, to the INNER MEANING, and to replace idolatry by MYSTIC COMMUNION [meditation] with the God who dwells WITHIN.

For this purpose he went to all the holy places, in Syria, Egypt, Greece and Spain; he even reached the rock of Gades, which later was to become Cadiz, [near southern tip of Spain, near Gibraltar] which was, according to Pliny, the last part of the continent that escaped the catastrophe of ATLANTIS. His travels also brought him as far as Gaul. However his chief work of religious reform was in Greece.

When Apollonius came to Ephesus, the citizens left their work and followed him, paying homage and applause. The first discourse of Apollonius given at Ephesus was from the porch of the temple of Diana, after the manner of the Stoics, exhorting them to spend their time in study and philosophy (spirituality) and to abandon their dissipations and cruel sports. He also preached on "Community of Goods" (`communism') illustrating his discourse with the parable of the sparrows.*

*While discoursing one day in one of the covered walks of Ephesus, on mutual aid and the advantages of `communism,' it chanced that a number of sparrows were sitting on a tree nearby in perfect silence. Suddenly another sparrow flew up and began chirping, as though it wanted to tell the others something. Whereupon the little fellows all set to chirping also, and flew away from the newcomer. Apollonius's superstitious audience were greatly struck by this conduct of the sparrows, and thought it was an augury of some important matter. But the philosopher continued his sermon, pointing out that the sparrow had invited it's friends to a banquet. Thereupon a boy slipped down a lane nearby and spilt some corn he was carrying in a bowl; then he picked up most of it and went away. The little sparrow, chancing on the scattered grains, immediately flew off to invite his friends to the feast. Most of the crowd then went off at a run to see if it were true; and when they came back shouting and all excited with wonderment, Apollonius spoke as follows:

"Ye see what care the sparrows take of one another, and how happy they are to share with all their goods. And yet we men do not approve; nay, if we see a man sharing his goods with other men, we call it wastefulness, extravagance and such names, and dub the men to whom he gives a share, fawners and parasites. What then is left to us except to shut us up at home like fattening birds, and gorge out bellies in the dark until we burst with fat?"

While delivering another lecture in Ephesus, Apollonius displayed his unusual clairvoyant power by observing an event occurring far away. In the midst of his discourse he beheld the murder of Domitian in Rome; and suddenly stopping his discourse, he cried out, "Keep up your spirits, O Ephesians, for this day the tyrant is killed. Then he told the astonished people what he had seen, namely that Domitian had been attacked by Stephanus and wounded; afterwards, as Philostratus tells us, "his bodyguards, hearing the noise, and concluding that all is not well, rushed into the closet and finding the tyrant fainting, put an end to his life."

Philostratus describes this incident as follows:

"At first he sank his voice as though in some apprehension; he however, continued his exposition but haltingly, and with far less force than usual, as a man who had some other subject in his mind than that on which he is speaking; finally he ceased speaking altogether as though he could not find his words. Then staring fixedly on the ground, he started forward three or four paces, crying out: `Strike the tyrant, strike!' And this, not like a man who sees an image in a mirror, but as one with an actual scene before his eyes, as though he were himself taking part in it."*

[*It must be understood that Domitian, a degenerate tyrant, was responsible for the most terrible atrocities committed against spiritual/philosophical personages, and was determined to stamp out by persecution all of the higher spiritual knowledge, which Apollonius wished to spread. It is in this context of the greater spiritual good of the whole human race that Apollonius was relieved at the news of the tyrant's death. On an individual level he would undoubtedly have the same compassion for him as a soul, as to any other man.]

Turning to his astonished audience, he told them what he had seen. But though they hoped it were true, they refused to believe it, and thought that Apollonius had taken leave on his senses. But the philosopher gently answered:

"You, on your part, are right to suspend your rejoicings till the news is brought you in the usual fashion; as for me, I go to return thanks to the Gods for what I have myself seen."

While at Ephesus, Apollonius predicted that the city would be afflicted with a plague; and later, when visiting Smyrna, emissaries came to him from Ephesus, begging him to rescue the people from this terrible scourge. "When he heard this," writes Philostratus, he said, 'I think the journey is not to be delayed; and no sooner had he uttered the words, than he was at Ephesus."

It was to this occurrence that Aelian referred as among the charges on which Apollonius was to be arraigned at his trial before Domitian in Rome, for when he appeared among the unhappy plague-stricken Ephesians, he reassured them, promising that he would put a stop to the plague, which promise he fulfilled. It is said that Apollonius stayed the plague in Ephesus by destroying a 'demon' in the guise of an old beggar-man.

As the result of his presence and labor in behalf of the people, the city of Ephesus, which was so notorious for its frivolity, was brought back by the teaching of Apollonius to the cultivation of philosophy and the practice of virtue. On this subject, Lecky, in his "History of European Morals," writes:

"Apollonius was admired at Ephesus; the 'devils' themselves contributed to his popularity by their oracles, which they gave out in his favor. It is claimed that he reclaimed the city from idleness, from a love of dancing, and from other fooleries to which it was addicted and that he endeavored to bring the inhabitants to be friendly to one another. He labored, in like manner in the other cities of Ionia to reform the manners of the people, and to establish unity amongst them."

In visiting the temples, advising with the priests and lecturing to the people, Apollonius spent his time in Ephesus. He also traveled to other cities of Ionia, adjacent to Ephesus, where he addressed the people. Everywhere he was received with demonstrations of joy and reverence. The people flocked to hear him, and many were benefited by his preaching and healing. The priests and oracles of Colphon and Didymus had already declared in his favor, and all persons who stood in need of assistance were commanded by the oracle to repair to Apollonius, such being the will of Apollo and the Fates. Embassies were sent from all the principal cities of Ionia offering him rights of hospitality. Smyrna sent ambassadors, who, when questioned for a reason of the invitation, replied, "I will come; our curiosity is mutual."

Arriving in Smyrna, the Ionians who were engaged in their Panon festival came out to meet him. He found the people given up to idle disputings, and much divided in their opinions upon all subjects which tended for the public welfare and the good government of the city. He exhorted them in their disputes to rather vie with each other in giving the best advice or in discharging most faithfully the duties of citizens, in beautifying their city with works of art and graceful buildings.

Apollonius delivered many discourses at Smyrna, always confining himself to such topics as were most useful to his hearers. He was the guest of Theron the elder, a stoic and an astronomer.

Entering Athens, Apollonius was recognized and acknowledged by the people as he approached and passed through the crowd, amid greetings and acclamations of joy, regardless of the sacredness of the occasion. When he entered the temple and applied for initiation into the mysteries, Apollonius was refused by the hierophant on the ground that he was an 'enchanter.' In reply Apollonius named the successor to the office of the hierophant who, he foresaw, would initiate him at some future date, which prediction was subsequently fulfilled.

While delivering a lecture in Athens, Apollonius's discourse was interrupted by a youth, who gave way to inane laughter, whom he found to be under demoniacal possession. Apollonius stopped his talk and commanded the demon [rebellious astral spirit - usually earthbound] to go out of the youth, and to give a sign of his departure. This soon occurred to the astonishment of the audience. The youth afterwards followed a philosophical mode of life.

Hearing of the frivolities with which the Athenians were now accustomed to celebrate the Dionysia, Apollonius rebuked them by reminding them of the exploits of their ancestors and of their legendary connection with Boreas the most masculine of the winds. [Appealing to their higher spiritual nature, in other words]. Another abuse which he arrested at Athens was the introduction of the gladiatorial exhibitions.

Part 8   Visit to the Gymnosophists

We now come to Apollonius's visit to the "Gymnosophists" of upper Egygt, whom Damis calls the "naked Egyptian philosophers," though according to Mead,* the word "naked" probably meant "lightly clad." That they might have been originally Buddhist missionaries who traveled westward is indicated by a statement by one of the younger members of the community who left it to follow Apollonius. He related that he came to join the community from the enthusiastic account of his father who told him that these "Ethiopians" were from India; and so he had joined them instead of making the long and perilous trip to the Indus in search of wisdom. If this is true, these Gymnosophists must have originally been Buddhist missionaries who traveled westward and settled in Egypt, recruiting members from the Egyptians, Arabs, and Ethiopians, and so in the course of time forgot their origin. This explains the great similarity of Gymnosophical, Essenian and Therapeut doctrines to Buddhist ones, aside from the direct importation of Buddhist teachings by Pythagoras and Apollonius.*

(*According to Mead, the Gymnosophists, were really a sect of advanced Essenes, or Therapeuts, as described by Philo in his "On the Contemplative Life," the description that Philo gives of the Therapeut community he visited on the shore of Lake Mareoris near Alexandria corresponding almost exactly with Damis's description of the Gymnosophist community in Upper Egypt. Both show the following unmistakable signs of Buddhist influence and origin.

(1) In both cases the members gave away all their worldly possessions before joining the community.

(2) There was a novitiate period and an initiation into the order,

(3) Abstinence from meats and wines was compulsory,

(4) Both practiced the healing art,

(5) Both made community of property the rule,

(6) Both took oaths of chastity and poverty;

(7) Both adopted and raised the children of strangers and orphans.

Indeed, the Gymnosophical community that Apollonius visited could very well have been one of the Therapeut communities described by Philo and which he visited at about the same period.* [*See the books by Arthur Lillie ("Buddhism in Christianity" and "India in Primitive Christianity") for details on the contribution of travelling Buddhist monks to Palestine, Egypt, Syria and Asia Minor, to the formation of the early Essene/Therapeut/Nazarite communities in these areas, which later became the base upon which Christianity was raised. A large number of the volumes in the Library of Alexandria were likewise of Buddhist origin.

According to Mead, this Gymnosophical community was originally of Buddhist origin, having been established by Buddhist monks. The origin of the Essene and Therapeut doctrines has been traced by some of the Buddhist missionaries sent out in the middle of the third century B.C. by ASHOKA, Buddhist Emperor of India, who traveled to Syria, Egypt, Macedonia and those parts of Asia Minor where the Essene communities were later known to exist. While it is possible that these communities may have existed previously and have been of Orphic and Pythagorean origin, it is probable that these Buddhist missionaries found in them a responsive audience.

Mead writes, "Just as some would ascribe the constitution of the Essene and Therapeut communities to Pythagorean influence, so others would ascribe their origin to Buddhist propaganda; and not only would they trace this influence to the Essene tenets and practices, but they even refer to the general teachings of the Christ to a Buddhist source in a Jewish monotheistic setting. Not only so but some would have it that two centuries before the direct general contact of Greece with India, brought about by the conquests of Alexander - INDIA, through Pythagoras, strongly and lastingly influenced all subsequent Greek thought.")

On the borderland between Egypt and Ethiopia, Apollonius praised an Egyptian youth, Timasio, for his continence, regarding him as of more merit than Hippolytis, because, while living chastely, he nevertheless does not speak or think of the divinity of Aphrodite [reproductive energies] otherwise than with respect.

Asked by the Gymnosophical philosophers to explain his Wisdom, Apollonius humbly replied that Pythagoras was the inventor of it, though he derived it from the Brahmans. This Wisdom, he added, had spoken to him in his youth, and had said:

"For sense, young sir, I have no charms; my cup is filled with toils unto the brim. Would anyone embrace my way of life, he must resolve to banish from his board all food that once bore life, to lose the memory of wine, and thus no more to wisdom's cup befoul -- the cup that doth consist of wine -- untainted souls. Nor shall wool warm him, nor aught that's made from an beast. I give my servants shoes of bast; and they sleep as they can. And if I find them overcome with love's delights, [lust] I've ready to pits down into which that justice which doth follow hard on wisdom's foot doth drag and thrust them; indeed, so stern am I to those who choose my way, that e'en upon their tongues I bind a chain.

"An innate sense a fitness and of right, and ne'er to feel that anyone's lot is better than thine own; tyrants to strike with fear instead of being a fearsome slave to tyranny; to have the Gods more greatly bless their scanty gifts than those who pour before them blood of bulls. If thou are pure, I'll give thee how to know what things will be as well, and fill thy eyes so full of Light, that thou may'st recognize the Gods the heroes know, and prove and try the shadowy forms that feign the shapes of men."

In thus addressing the Gymnosophists, Apollonius spoke to philosophers who lived just as he did, for these Egyptian sages ate no foods of animal origin, and were strict vegetarians as were the Brahman sages of the Himalayas, the wise men of the east, whom he had formerly visited.

A very interesting Socratic dialogue took place between Thespesion, the abbot of the Gymnosophist community and Apollonius on the comparative merits of the Greek and Egyptian ways of representing the gods. Inquiring of Apollonius whether Phidias and Praxiteles went up to heaven and took impression of the forms of the gods and then reproduced them in matter, Apollonius replied that imagination is the vision of higher realities or divine archetypes of things, and that each man has his higher Self - his angel of god-like beauty, which, like the gods, inhabits a heavenly world.

The Greek sculptors, he concluded, succeeded in reproducing these higher realities, which Pythagoras and Plato considered to be the true beings of things. Said Apollonius, "Imagination is a workman wiser far than imitation; for imitation only makes what it has seen, whereas imagination makes what it has never seen, conceiving it with reference to the thing it really is. Imagination is one of the most potent faculties, for it enables us to reach nearer to realities."

Thereupon, Thespesion stated that the Egyptians on the other hand, dare not give any precise form to the gods; and so they represent them only in symbols to which an occult meaning is attached. Thus arose the representation of the gods by different animal forms.

To this Apollonius replied that the danger is that the common people might worship these symbols and get unbeautiful ideas of the gods. The best thing would be to have the worshipper conform and fashion for himself an image of the object of his worship WITHOUT an external representation or idol.*

(*Concerning this dialogue, Mead comments as follows: "Apollonius, a priest of a universal religion, might have pointed out the good side and the bad side of both Greek and Egyptian religious art, and certainly taught the higher way of symbol-less worship, but he would not champion one popular cult against another." (Mead: "Apollonius of Tyana)

On his return from Egypt, Apollonius signified his approval of the conduct of Titus after he had taken Jerusalem, in refusing to accept a crown from the neighboring nations. Titus, who was then associated with his father in the government, invited Apollonius to Argos, and consulted him as to his future behavior as a ruler. Apollonius said that he would send him to his companion, Demetrius the Cynic, as a counsellor, which Titus, though the name, Cynic, was at first disagreeable to him, assented to with good grace. At another time he consulted with Apollonius privately on his destiny.

Though they had the best intellect of the Roman Empire from which to choose, the Emperor Vespasian and his son Titus preferred to consult Apollonius for advice concerning the management of their empire. In his last letter to Titus, Vespasian confesses that they were what they were solely owing to the good advice of Apollonius.*

(*Apollonius was wiser than most men because he derived his wisdom from a higher source, from the gods; this was expressed in one word by Apollonius in his answer to the Consul Telesinus, who asked him, "And what is your wisdom?" "An inspiration," replied the sage.)

On one occasion, Vespasian traveled from Rome to Egypt to ask Apollonius's advice on political matters. He found the sage seated in a temple. Approaching him, and apologizing for his intrusion, the emperor, an ardent admirer of the philosopher, said, "You have the amplest insight into the will of the gods and I do not wish to trouble the gods against their will."

On this occasion, Apollonius gave his august visitor a fine example of his prophetic and clairvoyant powers. He said, "O Zeus, this man who stands before thee is destined to raise afresh unto thee the temple which the hands of malefactors have set on fire." At that moment the temple in Rome was in flames, a fact which was verified by Vespasian later.

Part 9   *the Trials of Apollonius by Nero and Domitan*

During the reign of Nero, the philosophic cloak was proceeded against in the law-courts as the guise of diviners. Not to mention other cases, Musonius, a man second only to Apollonius, was imprisoned on account of his philosophy and came near to losing his life. Before Apollonius and his company reached the gates of Rome, a certain Philolaus of Citium tried to deter them from proceeding. To Apollonius this seemed a divinely ordained test to separate the stronger disciples from the weaker (whom, however, he did not blame); so that, out of thirty-four, only eight remained with him, the rest making various excuses for their flight at once from Nero and from philosophy.

Entering Rome, Apollonius publicly denounced the reigning tyranny, as one so grievous that under it men were not permitted to be wise. His discourses being all public, no accusations were made against him for a time. He spoke to men of standing in the same manner as to the common people. A public protest against luxury, delivered on a feast-day in a gymnasium which the Emperor was opening in person, led to his expulsion from Rome by Nero's minister Tegellinus, who henceforth kept a close watch on Apollonius.

His opportunity came at last when there was an epidemic of colds and the temples were full of people making supplicants for the Emperor, because he had a sore throat and the "divine voice" was hoarse. Apollonius, bursting with indignation at the folly of the multitudes remained quiet, but tried to calm a disciple by telling him to pardon the gods if they delight in buffoons."

This saying reported to Tigellinius, he had him arrested. Bringing him to trial, however, he found himself baffled, and in fear of his superhuman powers, let him go. Philostratus tells us that at his trial, "an informer, well instructed, came forward, who had been the ruin of many. He held in his hand a scroll wherein was written the accusation, which he flourished about him like a sword before the eyes of Apollonius, boasting that he had given it a sharp edge, and that now his hour had come. Upon this Tegellinus enfolded the scroll, when, lo, and behold, neither letter nor character was to be seen…All these things appeared, in the eyes of Tigellinus, divine, and above human power, and to show he did not wish to contend with a god, he bid him go where he pleased as he was too strong to be subject to authority."

When Domitian ascended the throne and began to show the same morbid vanity and cruelty which had characterized Nero, we find Apollonius traveling up and down the Empire, spreading seeds of discontent and rebellion against the crowned monster. To Domitian, he fearlessly said, "I am Apollo's subject not thine."*

(* How much different from the more compromising Christian messiah, who proved much more acceptable to Constantine's and his court, preaching as he did to "render unto Caesar the things that are Caesar's," doctrine which was the opposite of that preached by the revolutionary Apollonius, an enemy to tyranny. This makes it clear why the Romans refused to accept Christianity so long as Apollonius was its head, and why immediately after his replacement by Jesus (at the Council of Nicea in the year 335 A.D.), a previously persecuted 'communist' cult of the poor and oppressed was elevated to become the imperial religion of the Roman emperors.)

Apollonius did not try to start a revolution (against tyranny) only in one place, but throughout the Empire. Wherever he went, revolutions arose. He went into Gaul, and there with Vindex, he raised the standard of revolt.*

(*There can be no doubt that Apollonius was behind Vindex's revolt in Gaul, in concert with the governor of Baetica. After his expulsion from Rome, Apollonius went to Spain to aid in the forthcoming revolt against Nero. This is conjectured by Damis from the three days' secret interview that Apollonius had with the Governor of the Province of Baetica, who came to Cadiz especially to see him, and whose last words to Apollonius were, "Farewell, and remember Vindex.")

In Chios and Rhodes he succeeded in bringing about political reforms. Later with Domitian, a second Nero, no less cruel than his predecessor, and even exceeding him, if that were possible, we find the ever active and fearless Apollonius going up and down from one end of the Roman Empire to the other, sowing everywhere the seeds of discontent and rebellion against the tyrant of Rome. Still later we find him fostering a conspiracy against Domitian in favor of the virtuous Nerva.

Discovering the plot against him, Domitian ordered Apollonius to be arrested, but even this did not deter him. When Vespasian was emperor, Apollonius supported and counselled him so long as he worthily tried to follow out his instructions, but when he deprived th&127 Greek cities of their privileges, he immediately rebuked the Emperor to his face. "You have enslaved Greece," he wrote him. "You have reduced a free people to slavery."

When under Domitian, Apollonius became an object of suspicion to the Emperor for criticizing his acts as he did the follies of Nero, instead of keeping away from Rome, he determined to brave the tyrant to his face. Crossing from Egypt to Greece and taking ship at Corinth, he sailed by way of Sicily to Puteoli and thence to the Tiber mouth, and so to Rome where he was tried and acquitted.

Apollonius always considered wisdom his sovereign mistress and defended liberty even under Domitian. He entertained no fears of his own life, for, although many philosophers were going into involuntary exile during Domitian's reign, Apollonius determined to remain and take up arms for the good of Rome against Domitian, as he had done against Nero, although well knowing that Domitian would condemn him to destruction. To the pleading of hid disciple, Demetrius, not to enter Rome at the risk of his life after Domitian threatened to imprison and put to death any philosopher that remained in the city or attempted to enter it, Apollonius replied:

"I have raised the standard of liberty, and at the moment she is on trial -- shall I desert her? If so, of what friendship am I worthy after having thus betrayed my friends into the hands of the executioner?...My life is not necessary; to go to Rome my conscience tells me is. I shall therefore be true to myself and shall face the tyrant...I go to Rome! For, as Phrasea Paetus used to say, I had rather be killed today than go into voluntary exile tomorrow."

Some of the sayings of Apollonius against Domitian, the successor of Nero to the throne of Rome, who surpassed even his predecessor in cruelty, having been recorded; we are told that he fell under suspicion through his correspondence with Nerva and his associates Ofitus and Rufus. When proceedings against them were begun, Apollonius addressed the following words to the statue of Domitian: "Fool! How little you know of the Fates [Law of Karma] and Necessity! He who is destined to reign after you, should you kill him, will come to life again."

This was brought to Domitian's ears by means of Euphrates. Foreknowing that the Emperor had decided on his arrest, Apollonius anticipated the summons by setting out with Damis for Italy. At Puteoli, he met Demetrius, who told him that he has been accused of "sacrificing a boy to get divinations for the conspirators;" and that the further charges against him were his strange dress and the worship that was said to have been paid him by certain people. Demetrius tried to dissuade his master from staying to brave the anger of a tyrant unmoved by the most just defense, but Apollonius replied that he intended to remain and answer the charges against him, for to flee from a legal trial would, he believed, have the appearance of self-condemnation. And whither could he flee? It must be beyond the limits of the Roman Empire. Should he then seek refuge with men who knew him already, to whom he would have to acknowledge that he has left his friends to be destroyed by an accusation which he has not dared to face himself?

Before the tribunal, Aelian, Domitian's prefect, accused Apollonius of being worshipped by men and thinking himself worthy of equal honors with the gods. Apollonius was thrown into prison, where he spent his time exhorting the prisoners to courage and raising their spirits. Brought before Domitian, he bravely defended Nerva, Rufus and Orfitus, whom Domitian, had imprisoned as conspirators. Domitian insisted that he should defend himself alone from the charges, and not the others who were condemned. Apollonius, rather than defend himself, declared them innocent and protested against the injustice of assuming their guilt before the trial.

Domitian replied, telling him that as regards his own defense, he could take what course he liked; and thereupon he ordered his beard and hair cut, and put him into fetters such as are reserved for the worst criminals. (A letter attributed to Apollonius in which he supplicatingly entreats the Emperor to release him from his bonds, Philostratus pronounced as spurious.)

Being uneasy about his master's fate in Domitian's prison, Damis was reassured by Apollonius who said, "There is no one who will put us to death."

"But when, sir," asked Damis, "will you be set at liberty."

"Tomorrow," answered he, "if it depended on the judge, and this instant if it depended on myself."

And without a word more, he drew his leg out of the fetters, and said to Damis, "You will see the liberty I enjoy, and therefore I request you will keep up your spirit." He then put his leg back into the fetters.

While in prison, Domitian sent a Saracusan, who was his "eye and tongue," to Apollonius, telling him that he could gain his release if he gave information about the supposed conspiracy against the Emperor, but he had to leave without result. Apollonius then sent Damis to Puteoli, to expect with.Demetrius his appearance there, after he had made his defense.

Among the charges that Domitian made against Apollonius were the following:

Charge lst: With wearing garments which differ from those of other men, thereby attracting crowds of boisterous people to the detriment of the good order of the city. Of wearing the hair long and of living not in accord with good society.

Charge 2nd: With allowing and encouraging men to call him a god.

Brought before the tribunal, Apollonius disregarded the monarch, and did not even glance at him. The accuser therefore cried out to him to look towards the god of all men," whereupon Apollonius raised his eyes to the ceiling, thus indicating, according to Philostratus, that he was looking to Zeus.

After his triumphant defense, which he made spontaneously, since he was not permitted to read the long defense he had previously prepared, Domitian acquitted him, asking him, however, to remain so that he could converse with him in private. Apollonius thanked him, but added the stern reproof:

"Through the wretches who surround you, cities and islands are filled with exiles, the continent with groans, the armies with cowardice, and the senate with suspicion." Then he suddenly disappeared from among them; and in the afternoon of the same day, he appeared to Damis and Demetrius at Puteoli, as he had promised, at a time when they despaired to ever see him again. [i.e., He disappeared from in front of the Emperor Domitian at Rome, and rematerialized 150 miles away in Puteoli.]

After he had slept, to rest from the recent strenuous events in Rome, Apollonius told his disciples that he was leaving for Greece. Demetrius was afraid that he would not be sufficiently hidden there, but Apollonius replied that if all the earth belonged to the tyrant, they that die in the open day had a better part than they that live in concealment. To those in Greece who asked him how he escaped, he merely said that his defense had been successful. Hence, when many coming from Italy related what had really happened, he was almost worshipped, being regarded as divine, especially because he had in no way boasted of the marvelous mode of his escape.

Appendix THE TREATISE OF EUSEBIUS[1]

Translated by F.C. Conybeare (1912)

I

So then, my dear friend, you find worthy of no little admiration the parallel which, embellished with many marvels, this author has drawn between the man of Tyana arid our own Saviour and teacher. For already against the rest of the contents of the "Lover of Truth " (Philalethes), for so he has thought fit to entitle his work against us, it would be useless to take my stand at present; because they are not his own, but have been pilfered in the most shameless manner, not only I may say in respect of their ideas, but even of their words and syllables, from other authorities.

Not but what these parts also of his treatise call for their refutation in due season; but to all intents and purposes they have, even in advance of any special work that might be written in answer to them, been upset and exposed beforehand in a work which in as many as eight books Origen composed against the book which Celsus wrote and--even more boastfully than the " Lover of Truth,"--entitled " True Reason." The work of Celsus is there subjected to an examination in an exhaustive manner and on the scale above mentioned by the author in question, who in his comprehensive survey of all that anyone has said or will ever say on the same topic., has forestalled any solution of your difficulties which I could offer.

To this work of Origen I must refer those who in good faith and

---

[1] The following treatise was written by Eusebius Pamphilus of Caesarea in the fourth century

with genuine "love of truth" desire accurately to understand my own position. I will therefore ask you for the present to confine your attention to the comparison of Jesus Christ with Apollonius which is found in this treatise called the " Lover of Truth," without insisting on the necessity of our meeting the rest of his arguments, for these are pilfered from other people. We may reasonably confine our attention for the present to the history of Apollonius, because Hierocles, of all the writers who have ever attacked us, stands alone in selecting Apollonius, as he has recently done, for the purposes of comparison and contrast with our Saviour.

II

I NEED not say with what admiring approval he attributes his thaumaturgic feats not to the tricks of wizardry, but to a divine and mysterious wisdom; and he believes they were truly what he supposes them to have been, though he advances no proof of this contention.

Listen then to his very words: "In their anxiety to exalt Jesus, they run up and down prating of how he made the blind to see and worked certain other miracles of the kind." Then after an interval he adds as follows: "Let us note however how much better and more sensible is the view which we take of such matters, and explain the conception which we entertain of men gifted with remarkable powers." And thereupon after passing heedlessly by Aristeas of Proconnesus and Pythagoras as somewhat too old, he continues thus: " But in the time of our own ancestors, during the reign of Nero, there flourished Apollonius of Tyana, who from mere boyhood when he became the priest in Aegae of Cilicia of Asclepius, the lover of mankind, worked any number of miracles, of which I will omit the greater number, and only mention a few."

Then he begins at the beginning and enumerates the" wonders worked by Apollonius, after which he continues in the following words: "What then is my reason for mentioning these facts? It was in order that you may be able to contrast our own accurate and well-established judgment on each point, with the easy credulity of the Christians. For whereas we reckon him who wrought such feats not a god, but only a man pleasing to the gods, they on the strength of a few miracles proclaim their Jesus a god." To this he adds after a little more the following remark:"

And this point is also worth noticing, that whereas the tales of Jesus have been vamped up by Peter and Paul and a few others of the kind,--men who were liars and devoid of education and wizards, --the history of Apollonius was written by Maximus of Aegae, and by Damis the philosopher who lived constantly with him. and by Philostratus of Athens, men of the highest education, who out of respect for the truth and their love of mankind determined to give the publicity they deserved to the actions of a man at once noble and a friend of the gods." These are the very words used by Hierocles in his treatise against us which he has entitled "Lover of Truth."

III

Now Damis who spent -so much of his time with Apollonius was a native of Assyria, where for the first time, on his own soil, he came into contact with of him ; and he wrote an account of his intercourse with the person in question from that time onwards. Maximus however wrote quite a short account of a portion only of his career. Philostratus, however, the Athenian, tells us that he collected all the accounts that he found in circulation, using both the book of Maximus and that of Damis himself and of other authors; so he compiled the most complete history of any of this person's life, beginning with his birth and ending with his death.

IV

IF then we may be permitted to contrast the reckless and easy credulity which he goes out of his way to accuse us of, with the accurate and well-founded judgment on particular points of the Lover of Truth, let us ask at once, not which of them was the more divine nor in what capacity one worked more wondrous and numerous miracles than the other; nor let us lay stress on the point that our Saviour and Lord Jesus Christ was the only man of whom it was prophesied, thanks to their divine inspiration, by Hebrew sages who lived far back thousands of years ago, that he should once come among mankind; nor on the fact that he converted to his own scheme of divine teaching so many people; nor that he formed a group of genuine and really sincere disciples, of whom almost without exaggeration it can be said that they were prepared to lay down their lives for his teaching at a moment's call; nor that he alone established a school of sober and chaste living which has survived him all along; nor that by his peculiar divinity and virtue he saved the whole inhabited world, and still rallies to his divine teaching races from all sides by tens of thousands; nor that he is the only example of a teacher who, after being treated as an enemy for so many years, I might almost say, by all men, subjects and rulers alike, has at last triumphed and shown himself far mightier, thanks to his divine and mysterious power, than the infidels who persecuted him so bitterly, those who in their time rebelled against his divine teaching being now easily won over by him, while the divine doctrine which he firmly laid down and handed on has come to prevail for ages without end all over the inhabited world; nor that even now he displays the virtue of his godlike might in the expulsion, by the mere invocation of his mysterious name, of sundry troublesome and evil demons which beset men's bodies and souls, as from our own experience we know to be the case.

To look for such results in the case of Apollonius, or even to ask about them, is absurd. So we will merely examine the work of Philostratus, and by close scrutiny of it show that Apollonius was not fit to be classed, I will not say, among philosophers, but even among men of integrity and good sense, much less to be compared with our Saviour Christ, so far as we can depend on the work of a writer who, though according to the " Lover of Truth," he was highly educated, was in any case no respecter of truth. For such is his description of Philostratus the Athenian among others. In this way we shall easily appreciate the value of the rest of the authorities, who though, according to him, they were most highly educated, yet never by actual sifting of the facts, established them with any accuracy in the case of Apollonius. For when we have thoroughly examined these facts, we shall no doubt obtain a clear demonstration of the solidity and, as he imagines to himself, of the accuracy in detail of the condemnation which the " Lover of Truth," who has at the same time taken possession of the supreme courts all over the province, passes on Christians, and at the same time of what they are pleased to call our reckless and facile credulity, for we are accounted by them to be mere foolish and deluded mortals.

V

ANOTHER controversionalist, by way of beginning the affray, would without demur abuse and malign the man against whom he directed his arguments, on the ground that he was his enemy and adversary; I, however, my friend, used to regard the man of Tyana as having been, humanly speaking, a kind of sage, and I am still freely disposed to adhere to this opinion ; and I would like to set before you, if you ask it, my own personal opinion of him.

If anyone wishes to class him with any philosopher you like, and to forget all the legends about him and not bore me with them, I am quite agreeable. Not so if anyone ventures, whether he be Damis the Assyrian, or Philostratus, or any other compiler or chronicler, to overleap the bounds of humanity and transcend philosophy, and while repelling the charge of wizardry in word, yet to bind it in act rather than in name upon the man, using the mask of Pythagorean discipline to disguise what he really was. For in that case his reputation for us as a philosopher will be gone, and we shall have an ass instead concealed in a lion's skin; and we shall detect in him a sophist in the truest sense, cadging for alms among the cities, and a wizard, if there ever was one, instead of a philosopher.

VI

Do you ask me what I mean and what are my reasons for speaking thus? I will tell you. There are bounds of nature which prescribe and circumscribe the existence of the universe in respect of its beginnings and of its continuance and of its end, being limits and rules imposed on everything. By these this entire mechanism and edifice of the whole universe is constantly being brought to perfection ; and they are arranged by unbreakable laws and indissoluble bonds, and they guard and observe the all-wise will of a Providence which dispenses and disposes all things.

Now no one can change or alter the place and order of anything that has been once arranged; and if anyone is so venturesome as to wish to transcend his limits, he is restrained from transgressing divine law by the rule and decree of nature. So it is that the fish that lives in the waters is unable in defiance of nature to change on to dry land and live there; and on the other hand the creature bred on dry land will not plunge into the waters, and embrace there any permanent repose or abode ; nor by any huge leap can any tenant of earth raise himself aloft into the air, from a desire to soar about with the eagles ; and in turn, although of course the latter can alight upon the earth, by depressing and lowering their faculty of flight, and by relaxing the working of their wings, and renouncing the privilege of nature,--for this too is determined by the divine laws, namely that beings able to soar aloft are able to descend from on high,--yet the converse is not possible, so that the lowly habitant of earth should ever raise himself into the welkin.

In this way then the mortal race of men, while provided with soul and body, is yet circumscribed by divine bounds. Consequently he can never traverse the air with his body, however much he scorns to linger upon the paths of earth, without instantly paying the penalty neither of his folly; nor by spiritual exaltation can he in his thinking attain to the unattainable, without falling back into the disease of melancholy.

It is wisest then for him, on the one hand to transport his body along the ground with the feet given him for the purpose, and on the other hand to sustain his soul with education and philosophy. But he may well pray that some one may come to help him from aloft from the paths of heaven, and reveal himself to him as a teacher of the salvation that is there. For the following is a valid example to use as it is right for the physician to visit the sick, and for the teacher to accommodate himself to the, pupil who is entering upon his studies, and for a superior to quit his heights and condescend to the lowly, yet the converse is not right or possible. It follows then that there is no reason to prevent a divine nature, being beneficent and inclined to save and take providential care of things to come, from associating itself with men, for this is allowed also by the rule of divine providence; for according to Plato God was good, and no good being can ever feel any jealousy of any thing.

It follows that the controller of this universe, being good, will not care for our bodies alone, but much more for our souls, upon which he has conferred the privilege of immortality and free-will. On these then, as lord of the entire economy and of gifts of grace his bestowal of which will benefit our nature, he will, they being able to appreciate his bounty, bestow plenteously an illumination as it were of the light which streams from him, and will despatch the most intimate of his own messengers from time to time, for the salvation and succour of men here below. Of these messengers anyone so favoured by fortune, having cleansed his understanding and dissipated the mist of mortality, may well be described as truly divine, and as carrying in his soul the image of some great god.

Surely so great a personality will stir up the entire human race, and illuminate the world of mankind more brightly than the sun, and will leave the effects of his eternal divinity for the contemplation of future ages, in no less a degree affording an example of the divine and inspired nature than creations of artists made of lifeless matter. To this extent then human nature can participate in the super-human; but otherwise it cannot lawfully transcend its bounds, nor with its wingless body emulate the bird, nor being a man must one meddle with what appertains to demons.

VII

IN what light then, this being so, do you envisage for us Apollonius, my good compiler? If as a divine being and superior to a philosopher, in a word as one superhuman in his nature, I would ask you to keep to this point of view throughout your history, and to point me out effects wrought by his divinity enduring to this day.

For surely it is an absurdity that the works of carpenters and builders should last on ever so long after the craftsmen are dead, and raise as it were an immortal monument to the memory of their constructive ability; and yet that a human character claimed to be divine should, after shedding its glory upon mankind, finish in darkness its shortlived career, instead of displaying for ever its power and excellence. Instead of being so niggardly liberal to some one individual like Damis and to a few other short-lived men, it should surely make its coming among us the occasion of blessings, conferred on myriads not only of his contemporaries, but also of his posterity.

This I ween is how the sages of old raised up earnest bands of disciples, who continued their tradition of moral excellence, sowing in men's hearts a spirit truly immortal of progress and reform. If on the other hand you attribute to this man a mortal nature, take care lest by endowing him with gifts which transcend mortality, you convict yourself of fallacy and miscalculation.

VIII

BUT enough of this. His hero is introduced to us as a divine man, who assumes from birth the guise and personality of a demon of the sea. For he says that to his mother when she was about to bear her child, there appeared the figure of a demon of the sea, namely Proteus, who in the story of Homer ever changes his form. But she, in no way frightened, asked him what she would bring to birth; and he replied: " Myself." Then she asked: "And who are you? " "Proteus," he replied, " of Egypt." And then he writes about a certain meadow and about swans that assisted the lady to bear her child, though without telling us whence he derived this particular; for assuredly he does not attribute this story to Damis the Assyrian writer. But a little further on in the same history he represents Apollonius as using, in token of his being of a divine nature these very words to Damis himself: " I myself, my companion, understand all languages though I have learned none." And again he says to him:"

Do not be surprised, for I know what men are thinking about, even when they are silent." And again in the temple of Asclepius he was much honoured by the god, and is said to have possessed a certain natural gift of prescience, which he did not acquire by learning, from very childhood. We learn, in a word, that he was born superior to mankind in general, and so he is described from the first moment of his birth throughout his history.

Anyhow on one occasion after he had loosed himself from his bonds, his historian adds the remark : " Then Damis declares he for the first time clearly understood the nature of Apollonius, that it was divine and superior to humanity. For without offering any sacrifice,--for how could he offer one in the prison?--and without offering any prayer, without a single word, he just laughed at his fetters." And at the end of the bookl we learn that his grave was nowhere to be found on earth; but that he went to heaven in his physical body accompanied by hymns and dances. Naturally if he was so great as he is described in the above, he may be said "to have wooed philosophy in a more divine manner than Pythagoras, or Empedocles, or Plato." For these reasons we must surely class the man among the gods.

IX

WELL, we will not grudge him his natural and self-taught gift of understanding all languages. But if he possessed it, why was he taken to a school-master, and if he had never learnt any language whatever, why does his historian malign him and declare that, not by nature, but by dint of close study and application, he acquired the Attic dialect? For he tells us outright " that as he advanced in youth he displayed a knowledge of letters and great power of memory, and force of application, and that he spoke the Attic dialect." We also learn that "when he reached his fourteenth year his father took him to Tarsus, to Euthydemus of Phoenicia, who was a good rhetor, and gave him his education, while. Apollonius clung to his teacher." We further learn that " he had as fellow-students members of the school of Plato and of Chrysippus and members of the Peripatetic set. That he also diligently listened to the doctrines of Epicurus, because he did not despise even them, though he grasped the teachings of Pythagoras with a certain indescribable wisdom." So varied was the education of one who had never learnt any language, and who by his divine power anticipated "the thoughts of men even when they are silent."

X

AND after an interval our author again expresses his admiration at the ease with which Apollonius understood the language of animals, and he goes on to tell us the following: " And moreover he acquired of an understanding of the language of animals; and he learnt this, too, in the course of his travels through Arabia, where the inhabitants best know this language and practise it.

For the Arabians have a way of understanding without difficulty swans and other birds when they presage the future in the same way as oracles. And they get to understand the dumb animals by eating, so they say, some of them the heart and others the liver of dragons." In this instance, then, it seems anyhow to have been the case that the Pythagorean who abstained from animal food and could not even bring himself to sacrifice to the gods, devoured the heart and liver of dragons, in order to participate in a form of wisdom that was in vogue among the

Arabs. After learning under such masters, how could he attain to their accomplishments otherwise than by imitating their example? We must therefore add to the teachers whom we have already enumerated the sages of Arabia who taught him his knowledge of augury; and this no doubt inspired him subsequently to foretell what the sparrow meant when he called his fellows to a meal, and so to impress the bystanders with the idea that he had worked a mighty miracle. Arid in the same way when he saw the freshly-slain lioness with her eight whelps by the side of the road which led into Assyria, he immediately conjectured from what he saw the length of their future stay in Persia, and made a prophecy thereof.

XI

AND in just keeping with his visits to the Arabians were the studies he undertook among the Persians also, according to the account given by the same author. For after forbidding Damis, so we are told, to go to the magi, though Damis was his only pupil and companion, he went alone to school with them at midday and about midnight; alone in order not to have as his companion in the study of magic one who was clearly without a taste for such things. And again when he came to converse with Vardan the Babylonian king, it is related that he addressed him as follows: "My system of wisdom is that of Pythagoras, a man of Samos, who taught me to worship the gods in this way and to recognize them, whether they are seen or unseen, and to be regular in converse with the gods." Who can possibly allow this to be true of him, seeing that Pythagoras himself has left no scripture of the kind, nor any secret writings, such that we can even suspect him to have had such resources at his disposal?

As for his teacher of the Pythagorean philosophy, it is testified that he was in no way better than the Epicureans by Philostratus himself, who speaks of him as follows: "He had as a teacher of the system of Pythagoras not a very good man, nor one who put his philosophy into practice; for he was the slave of his belly and his desires and modelled his life on that of Epicurus. And this man was Euxenus of Heraclea in Pontus. But he had a good acquaintance with the tenets of Pythagoras, just as birds have of what they learn to say from men." What ridiculous nonsense to pretend that Apollonius can have derived from this man, his gift of conversing with the gods. But let us for the moment admits that there were other expounders of the system from whom he may have learned, although the author anyhow gives no hint of any such thing.

Still we must ask : was there then ever any one of these teachers that professed either to know himself, by having learnt from Pythagoras personally, or to teach others., how to recognize and frequent in their conversations gods, whether seen or unseen ? Why, even the famous Plato, although more than anyone else he shared in the philosophy of Pythagoras, and Archytas too, and Philolaus the one man who has handed down to us in writing the conversations of Pythagoras, and any others who were disciples of the philosopher and have handed down to his posterity his opinions and tenets in writing, -- none of these ever boasted of any such form of wisdom. It follows then that he learnt these things not from Pythagoras, but from other sources; and with a wilful affectation of solemnity he only labels himself with the philosopher's name But admitting, though it is against all probability, that he is not lying, but telling the truth, we are still at a loss to know, how he can pretend to have acquired this lore from the Samian himself above mentioned, inasmuch as the latter deceased some thousand years before him.

Therefore we must reckon among the Arabians this teacher also who communicated to him a knowledge of the gods of so mysterious character as he imagines this to be. If then he was of a divine nature, it follows that the story of his teachers is a pure fiction. On the other hand if the story was true, then the legend was false, and the allegation in the book that he was divine is devoid of all truth.

XII

I HAVE no wish to enquire curiously about the ghost of Proteus, or to ask for confirmation of it, nor to demand proof of his ridiculous story that swans surrounded his mother and assisted her to bring him into the world ; equally little do I ask him to produce evidence of his fairy-tale about the thunderbolt ; for as I said before he cannot anyhow claim the authority of Damis for these particulars, inasmuch as the latter joined him much later on in the city of Nineveh of Assyria. I am however quite ready to accept all that is probable and has an air of truth about it, even though such details may be somewhat exaggerated and highly-coloured out of compliment to a good man ; for I could still bring myself to accept them, as long as they are not bewilderingly wonderful and full of nonsense.

I do not therefore mind the author telling us that Apollonius was of an ancient family and lineally descended from the first settlers, and was rich, if it were so, beyond all other people of that region: and that when he was young he not only had the distinguished teachers mentioned, but, if he likes, I will allow that he became himself their teacher and master in learning. I grant too, in addition, that he was skilful in ordinary matters, and so was able by giving the best of advice to rid of his malady one who had come to the temple of Asclepius in order to be healed.' For we read that he suggested to a man afflicted with dropsy a regime of abstinence well suited to cure his disease, and in that way restored him to health : and so far we must needs commend the youthful Apollonius for his good sense.

On another occasion he very properly excluded from the temple a man who was notorious for his wickedness, although he was prepared to offer the most expensive sacrifices, for he represents the man in question as the richest and most distinguished of all the people of his region. Nor would anyone object to his being classed among the temperate, inasmuch as he repelled with insults a lover who designed to corrupt his youth, and also, as the narrative informs us, kept himself throughout pure of intercourse with women.

We can also believe the story of his keeping silence for five years in the spirit of Pythagoras; and the way moreover in which he accomplished this vow of silence was praiseworthy. All this and the like is merely human, and in no way incongruous with philosophy or with truth, and I can therefore accept it, because I set a very high value upon candour and love of truth. Nevertheless to suppose that he was a being of superhuman nature, and then to contradict this supposition at a moment's warning, and to forget it almost as soon as it is made--this I regard as reprehensible and calculated to fasten a suspicion not only on the author, but yet more on the subject of his memoir.

XIII

THESE particulars we have taken from the first book of Philostratus; and let us now go on to consider the contents of the second. The story takes him on his travels and brings him from Persia to India. He next shows a want of good taste by relating, as if it were a miracle, how Apollonius and his companions saw some sort of demon, to which he gives the name of Empusa, along the road, and of how they drove it away by dint of abuse and bad words. And we learn that when some animals were offered them for food, he told Damis that he was quite willing to allow him and his companions to eat the flesh, for as far as he could see their abstinence from meat had in no way advanced their moral development, though in his own case it was imposed by the philosophic profession he had made in childhood. And yet is it not incredible to anyone that he should not have hindered Damis, as his best friend., and as the only disciple and follower of his life, that he had, and the only one whom he was trying to convert to his philosophy, that he should not, I repeat, have tried to hinder him from consuming the flesh of living animals, that being an unholy food according to Pythagoras, and that instead of doing so, he should tell him for reasons inexplicable to me that it will do no good to himself, and admit that he saw no moral advantage in them produced by such abstinence ?

XIV

IN the next place I would have you notice what sort of samples of truth are set before us by this Philostratus to whose truthfulness Hierocles the self-styled Lover of Truth bears witness. For we are told that when Apollonius was among the Indians, he employed an interpreter, and through him held the conversation with Phraotes, for that was the name of the king of the Indians. Thus he, who just before, according to Philostratus, had an understanding of all languages, now, on the contrary, according to the same witness, is in need of an interpreter. And again, he who read the thoughts of men, and almost like their god Apollo

"Understood the dumb and heard him who spake not" has to ask, by means of an interpreter, what was the king's way of life, and he asks him to supply him with a guide on his journey to the Brahmans. And after an interval the other, who is king of the Indians, and a barbarian to boot, gets rid of the interpreter, and addresses Apollonius in Greek; and speaking in that language details to him his education and his wealth of learning. But Apollonius none the less neglected on this occasion to display, as he should have done, his own perfect acquaintance with their tongue.

XV

ON the contrary he is astonished to find the Indian talking Greek, as Philostratus consistently, it would seem, with himself, tells us in his book. For how could he be astonished thereat, unless he had regarded him as a barbarian? And in spite of his having admired him for what he was, he could never have expected him to talk Greek. In the sequel, as if he were astonished at some exhibition of the miraculous and were still unable to explain it, Apollonius says: "Tell me, O king, how you came to have such facility in the Greek tongue? And where did you get hereabouts the philosophy you possess? For I do not think that you can say you owe it to teachers anyhow, for it is not likely that the Indians have any teachers of this." Such are the wonderful utterances to which one, whose prescience included everything, gives vent; and the king answers them by saying that he had had teachers, and he tells him who they were, and relates all the particulars of his own history on his father's side.

Next we are told that the Indian had to judge between certain parties about a treasure which had been hunted up in a field, the question at issue being whether this field ought to be assigned to the seller or buyer of the place. Our supreme philosopher and darling of heaven is asked his opinion, and awards it to the purchaser, assigning his reason in these words: "That the gods would never have deprived the one of the land, if he had not been a bad man; nor would ever have given the other riches under the soil, unless he had been better than the seller."

We must conclude then, if we are to believe him, that men who are comfortably off and richer than their neighbours, are to be esteemed thrice happy and beloved of the gods, even though they should be the most shameless and abandoned of mankind; on the other hand only the poorest, say, even a Socrates, or a Diogenes, or the famous Pythagoras himself, or any other of the most temperate and fairest-minded of men, are to be esteemed ill-starred wretches. For if one follows the reasoning here used, one must allow that on its showing the gods would never have deprived the poor, that is to say, the very men who excel others, if judged by the standard of philosophy, even of a bare living and of the necessities of life, unless they had been utterly vile in character, and at the same time they have endowed those who are abandoned in their character with a plenty even of things that were not necessary to them, unless they proved themselves better than the others just mentioned; from which the absurdity of the conclusion is manifest to everyone.

XVI

AFTER setting before you these incidents out of the second book, let us pass on to the third, and consider the stories told of the far-famed Brahmans. For here we shall have to admit that the tales of Thule, and any other miraculous legends ever invented by any story-tellers, turn out to be by comparison with these quite reliable and perfectly true. It is anyhow worth our while to examine these, because this self-styled lover of truth has not scrupled to fasten on ourselves a charge of reckless credulity and levity of character, while claiming for himself and for those like him an accurate judgment, well based on an understanding of the fact. Note then the sort of miracles on which he prides himself, when he prefers Philostratus to our own divine evangelists, on the ground that he was not only a most highly educated man, but most attentive to the truth.

XVII

To begin with then, on the way to the Brahmans, Philostratus introduces us to a lady who met Apollonius, and who, from her head down to her loins, was wholly white in colour, while the rest of her person was black. The mountains again, as they went forward on the road to the Brahmans, were planted with pepper trees, and the apes cultivated the same; and then there were certain dragons of extraordinary size, from whose heads were thrown off sparks of fire, and if you slew one of them, he : says that you found marvellous stones upon the head rivalling the gem of Gyges, as mentioned in Plato. And all this was before they reached the hill on which the Brahmans lived. And when they reached this, we read that they saw there a well of sandarac, full of wonderful water, and hard by a crater of fire, from which there arose a lead-coloured flame ; and there were two jars there of black stone, the one of which contained rain, and the other winds, from which the Brahmans supply such people of the country as they are pleased to favour.

Besides this they found among them images of Athene Polias and of Apollo Pythius, and of Dionysus of the Lake and of certain other Hellenic gods. And the master of them all was named Iarchas, and they saw him sitting on a very lofty throne in a state of pomp that was far from philosophic, but rather appropriate to a satrap. And this throne was made of black bronze and was decorated with golden images, such as we might of course expect philosophers to fabricate when they take to working like base mechanics at forge and steel, even if they do not like conjurers make their handiwork to move by itself. But the thrones, upon which the rest of them, who were inferior teachers to him, were sitting, were, he says, of bronze, but not incised and not so high. For I suppose they could not help bestowing upon the teacher of so divine a philosophy the privilege of having images and gold on his throne, just as if he were a tyrant.

XVIII

AND we are told that Iarchas, the moment he saw Apollonius, addressed him by name in the Greek tongue, and asked him for the letter which he brought from Phraotes, for he had already received this by dint of his foreknowledge ; and by way of parading the inspired character of his prescience, he told him before he set eyes on the epistle, that it was one letter short, namely of a delta ; and he began at once in a vulgar manner in that very first interview, like a man who has got wealth for the first time and does not know how to use it, to show off his superiority as a seer, by running off the names of Apollonius' father and mother, and telling him all about his family and upbringing and education, and about his periodical voyages abroad, and about his journey thither to himself, and about what he had done himself or said to his companions on the road.

And next this wonderful author tells us that the " Brahmans, after anointing themselves together with Apollonius with an amber-like drug, took a bath, and then standing round as if in chorus, struck the earth with their staves, and the earth arched itself up and elevated them some two cubits into the air, so that they stood there levitated up in the air itself for some considerable length of time. And he relates that they drew down fire from the sun without any effort on their part and whenever they chose.

And the miracle-monger adds another marvel to these, when he tells that there were four tripods like those of Pytho which wheeled themselves forth, moving of their own accord; and he goes so far as to compare these to the tripods in Homer, and he says that there were set upon them cup-bearers to serve in the banquet, four in number and made of bronze. And in addition he tells us that the earth too strewed grass beneath them of her own accord and unasked. And of these tripods two, he says, ran with wine, and of the other two, the one supplied hot water and the other cold. And the cup-bearers of bronze drew for the guests in due mixture both the wine and the water, and pushed round the cups in a circle, just as they are handed round in a symposium.

XIX

SUCH are the stories which Hierocles, who has been entrusted to administer the supreme courts of justice all over the province, finds true and reliable after due enquiry, at the same time that he condemns us for our excessive credulity and frivolity ; and after himself believing such things when he finds them in Philostratus, he proceeds to brag about himself and says (I quote his very words): " Let us anyhow observe how much better and more cautiously we accept such things, and what opinion we hold of men gifted with such powers and virtues."

XX

IT was after such a symposium, according to the same Philostratus, that a king who was sojourning in India is introduced to drink with the philosophers; and we hear that he took occasion to insult philosophy with drunken jests, and that he got so tipsy in their presence as to hurl defiance at the Sun and brag about himself. All this we learn, and that Apollonius once more, by means of an interpreter, learned his history from him and conversed in turn with him, Iarchas interpreting between them. Surely it may well excite our wonder that so insolent a fellow and so great a buffoon was allowed to get drunk and show off his tipsy wit among such great philosophers, when he was unworthy even to be present at a meeting of philosophers, much less at the hearth of men who were equal to gods ?

But what possesses me to call them the peers of gods and chaff them about their dignity? Why, when Apollonius asked them whom they considered themselves to be, " Gods," answered Iarchas ; who, I suppose in his quality as god, as little as could be in the style of philosopher, save the mark, nay, surely betraying an equally scant respect for the dignity of the god whom he professed himself to be, set the example of drinking to his fellow-banqueters by stooping down over the bowl, which, as our author is careful to tell us, supplied plenty of drink for all of them, and refreshed itself, as do holy and mysterious wells for those who fill their pitchers from them.

XXI

AFTER this there was general conversation and some serious discussion among the philosophers, in the course of which Iarchas explained that his own soul had once been in the body of another man who was a king, and that in that state he had performed this and that exploit; while Apollonius told them that he had once been the pilot of a ship in Egypt, and had accomplished all sorts of exploits which he enumerated to them. Then they put questions to each other, and received answers, which in the name of wisdom have scant title to be recorded at all.

Thus we learn that Apollonius asked if they had any golden water among them. What a clever and marvellous question! And he also asked about men who live underground, and about others called pigmies, and shadow-footed men, and he asked if they had among them a four-footed animal called a martichora, which has a head like that of a man, but rivals a lion in size, while from its tail projects hairs like thorns a cubit long, which it is accustomed to shoot out like arrows at those who hunt it. Such then were the questions which Apollonius put to the sages, and Iarchas instructed him about the pigmies, and told him that they were indeed people dwelling underground, but spent their lives on the other side of the river Ganges ; but as to the other things which he asked about, Iarchas said that they never had existed at all.

XXII

AFTER that Philostratus described a wool which the earth grew for them to supply material for their dress, from which we must infer that these philosophers plied the loom and occupied themselves with spinning wool in order to make their raiment, for we do not hear of any woman being smuggled into their community; but perhaps he means that by a miracle the wool grew of its own initiative into their sacred garments. And we hear that each of them carried a staff and a ring which was imbued with mysterious power. There follow a series of miraculous performances on the part of the Brahman,--how for example he recalled to his senses by means of a letter one who was possessed with a demon, how by stroking a man who was lame he healed his dislocated hip, how he vouchsafed to restore a man's hand that was withered, and to a blind man gave sight.

Our blessings on an author who saves us so much trouble. Can we doubt that these stories are true, when his very insistence on the truth of his earlier tales, I refer to those of lightning and wind kept in jars, and of tripods of stone walking about of their own accord and of cupbearers of bronze passing round the cups in a circle, fully betrays and exposes the mythical character of everything else which he has to tell us. Philostratus moreover declares that Damis related how carefully Apollonius excluded himself from being present at the philosophical sessions which he held with Iarchas ; and he says that Apollonius was given by the latter seven rings which were called after the stars, and that he wore these one by one upon the days respectively called by their names.

Though we learn this much on this occasion from a gentleman who is esteemed by the Lover of Truth to have had a respect for facts, further on in his book, as if by way of condemning the wizardry of the Brahmans, and as if he was anxious to acquit Apollonius of the charge of having dabbled therein, he adds the following remark, which I repeat textually : " But when he saw among the Indians the tripods and the cup-bearers and the other figures which I have said entered of their own accord, he did not either ask how they were contrived, or desire to learn ; but although he praised them, he disclaimed any wish to imitate them." And how, my good fellow, did he disclaim any wish of the kind? Is this the man who was careful to exclude Damis from the philosophical seances he held with them, and who thought it his duty to conceal from his only companion all that he had done in those seances?

And how could he have disclaimed any wish to imitate them when he accepted the seven rings named after the stars, and held it needful to wear these all through the rest of his life upon the days severally named after them, and that although, as you say yourself, they had a secret power in them. Even if we grant that he did not aspire to imitate these inventions, it is clear that his disclaimer was not due to their being uncanny. How then could he praise things which he disdained to imitate? If he praised them, as being divinely operated, why did he not imitate things so praiseworthy? To crown all, on his return after he had stayed with them, we learn that he arrived with his companions at the country of the Oritae, where he found the rocks and the sand and the dust which the rivers bring down to the sea, all alike made of bronze.

XXIII

ALL this is contained in the third book of Philostratus, and let us now pass on to those which follow. We learn that when he had returned from the country of the Indians to the land of Hellas, the gods themselves proclaimed him to be the companion of the gods, inasmuch as they sent on to him the sick to be healed. And, indeed, as if his visit to the Arabs and to the Magi and to the Indians had turned him into some miraculous and divine being, our author, now that he has got him home again, plunges straight into a lengthy description of his miracles.

And yet one might fairly argue that if he had been of a diviner than merely human nature, then he ought long before, and not only now, after entering into relation with other teachers, to have begun his career of wonder-working; and it was superfluous for him to take so much trouble to acquire the multifarious lore of Arabs and of Magi and of Indians., if he was really what the initial assumption made by Philostratus assumes him to have been. But anyhow, according to this truth-loving author, we have now got him back again., ready to show off the wisdom which he has acquired from so great masters; and as one fresh from Arabia and equipped with the science of augury in vogue among the inhabitants of that country, he begins by interpreting to the bystanders what the sparrow wanted and intended when it summoned its fellows to their dinner. Next he has a presentiment of the plague in Ephesus, and warns the citizens of what is coming. And he himself sets before us in his Apology to Domitian the explanation of this presentiment. For when the latter asked him what was his prediction, he answered: " Because, my prince, I use a very light diet, I was the first to scent the danger."

And then he relates a third miracle of him, which was nothing less than that of his averting the plague. Although the author has been careful not to include this story in the final counts retained against Apollonius, probably because it was impossible for him to rebut a charge founded upon it by any defence which he could offer, we nevertheless will, if you will allow us, publish the story and give it full publicity, because our doing so will render needless any further criticism of it. For if anybody feels the shadow of doubt about the matter, the very manner in which the story is told will convince him that fraud and make-believe was in this case everything, and that if ever anything reeked of wizardry this did. For he pretends that the plague was seen in the form of an aged man, a beggar and dressed in rags ; who, when Apollonius ordered the mob to stone him, began by shooting fire from his eyes, but afterwards, when he had been overwhelmed by the stones thrown at him, he appeared as a dog all crushed and vomiting foam, as mad dogs do. And he writes that Apollonius mentioned this episode also in the defence he addressed to the autocrat Domitian, as follows: "

For the form of the plague--and it resembled an aged beggar--was both seen by me, and when I saw it I overcame it, not by staying the course of the disease, but by utterly destroying it." Who, I would ask, after reading this would not laugh heartily at the miracle-mongering of this thaumaturge? For we learn that the nature of the plague was a living creature and as such exposed at once to the eyes of the bystanders and to the showers of stones they hurled at it, and that it was crushed by men, and vomited foam, when all the time a plague is nothing in the world but a corruption and vitiation of the atmosphere, the circumambient air being changed into a morbid condition composed of noxious and evil exhalations, as medical theory teaches us. And on other grounds, too, this story of the phantom plague can be exploded; for the story tells us that it only afflicted the city of Ephesus, and did not visit the neighbouring populations; and how could this not have been the case, if the surrounding atmosphere had undergone vitiation ? for the infection could not have been confined to one spot, nor have beset the air of Ephesus alone.

XXIV

THE fourth wonder which he relates is how the soul of Achilles appeared close by his own sepulchre, dressed the first time in a tunic, and five cubits high, and subsequently growing till it was twelve cubits in stature, and accusing the Thessalians for not continuing according to custom to offer him the due funeral rites, and furthermore still nursing wrath against the Trojans for the wrongs which they had committed against him, and bidding Apollonius ask him questions on five topics, such as he himself might desire to learn about, and the Fates permit him to know of.

We next learn that the omniscient one, who boasted of his prescience of future events, was still ignorant of whether Achilles had been buried, and of whether the Muses and Nereids had bestowed their dirges upon him. And accordingly he asked Achilles about these matters, and enquires most earnestly whether Polyxena had been slain over his tomb, and whether Helen had really come to Troy, --questions surely of a most solemn kind, and such as to stimulate others to lead the philosophical life of the hero, besides being in themselves of much importance. Thereupon he falls to wondering if there had ever been among the Hellenes so many heroes all at one time, and whether Palamedes had ever reached Troy. Surely it was disgraceful in the extreme that one who was the companion of gods, whether seen or unseen, should know so little of such matters as to need to ask questions again and again about them?

Unless, indeed, because in this scene he is introduced as associating with the dead, the author intentionally gives a frigid turn to his questions, in order to avert the suspicion of his having irreligiously pryed into the secrets of magic. For we may notice he represents him as arguing in his Apology that there was no colour of necromancy in the manner in which the spectre appeared to him, and says: " For without digging any trench like Odysseus, and without tempting the souls of the dead with the blood of lambs, I managed to converse with Achilles, merely by using the prayers which the Indians declare we ought to make use of in addressing heroes." This is how Apollonius now brags to his companion, although our author testifies that he had learned nothing from the Indians nor felt attracted by their wisdom.

XXV

WHAT then is the reason, my good fellow, supposing that there was no devilish curiosity here at work, why he would not allow Damis, whom you admit to have been his sole and genuine companion, to share with him in this marvellous vision and interview? And why, too, was he not able to do all this by daytime, instead of doing it in the dead of night and alone? Why, too, did the mere cry of the cocks drive away the soul of the hero? For he says, "It vanished with a mild flash of lightning, for indeed the cocks were already beginning to crow." I cannot but think that evil demons would have found such an hour seasonable and appropriate for their devilish interviews, rather than the soul of a hero which, having been freed from the crass matter of the body, must necessarily be good and unsullied.

In any case the demon conjured up on this occasion is represented as of a malignant and envious disposition, both rancorous and mean in humour. For how else can we characterise one who drove away Antisthenes, a poor youth so serious that he was endeavouring to become a follower of the philosopher Apollonius? For Achilles insists that he shall not initiate him in his philosophy, and he adds the reason: "For," says he, " he is too much of a descendant of Priam, and the praise of Hector is never out of his mouth." And how could he be other than rancorous and mean; if he was wrath with the Thessalians for not sacrificing to him, and still refused to be reconciled to the Trojans, because thousands of years before they had sinned against him, and that although the latter were continually sacrificing and pouring out libations to him ? The only exception is that he ordered Apollonius to restore the tomb of Palamedes, which together with his statue had fallen into decay.

XXVI

THE fifth and sixth miracles however in this book do not stand in need of much argument and discussion, so thoroughly do they prove our writer's easy credulity. For Apollonius, as they say, drives out one demon with the help of another. The first of the demons is expelled from an incorrigible youth, while the second disguises itself by assuming the form of a woman: and the latter our clever author calls by no other names than those of Empusa and Lamia. As for the damsel whom he is said subsequently to have brought back again to life in Rome after she had died, the story clearly impressed Philostratus himself as being extremely incredible, and we may safely reject it. Anyhow he hesitates and doubts, whether after all a spark of life might have not lingered on in the girl unnoticed by her attendants. For he says that according to report "it was raining at the time, and a vapour exhaled from the face of the girl."

Anyhow if such a miracle had really been wrought in Rome itself, it could not have escaped the notice first of the emperor and after him of his subordinate magistrates, and least of all of the philosopher Euphrates who at the time was in the country and was staying in Rome, who indeed, as we learn later on, is related to have launched against Apollonius the accusation of being no other than a wizard. It would certainly too, had it actually occurred, have been included by the accuser among the other charges levelled against him.

Well, just these and no more are the more particular and special achievements of Apollonius, although there are a myriad other cases in the book in which his sooth-sayings and prophecies are set down to his gift of foreknowledge; and we learn that at Athens, when he desired to be initiated in the Eleusinian mysteries, the priest there would not admit him, and declared that he would never initiate a wizard nor throw open the Eleusinian mysteries to a man who was addicted to impure rites. We also hear about a lewd fellow who went begging about Rome, rehearsing the songs of Nero on his lyre for pay; and we are told that this most philosophic of teachers out of fear of Nero ordered his companions to bestow alms on him in recognition of his clever accomplishments.

XXVII

SUCH are the contents of the fourth book, and in the fifth book of his history, after a few remarks about his gift of prescience, our author is so lost in admiration as to add the following remark, which I repeat textually. "That then he was enabled to make such forecasts by some divine impulse, and that it is no sound inference to suppose, as some people do, that Apollonius was a wizard, is clear from what I have said. But let us consider the following facts: wizards, whom for my part I reckon to be the most unfortunate of mankind, claim to alter the course of destiny, either by tormenting the ghosts whom they encounter, or by means of barbaric sacrifices, or by means of certain incantations or anointings.

But Apollonius himself submitted to the decrees of the Fates, and foretold that they must, needs come to pass; and his foreknowledge was not due to wizardry, but derived from what the gods revealed to him. And when among the Indians he beheld their tripods, and their dumb waiters and other automata which I described as entering the room of their own accord, he neither asked how they were contrived, nor wished to learn.

He only praised them, but did not aspire to imitate them." Such a passage as the above clearly exhibits in the light of wizards the famous philosophers of India. For notice that when he is arguing about wizards, he mentions them too and says that their marvels were cleverly contrived indeed, but that his hero held himself carefully aloof from such their contrivances, on the ground that they were not moral. If therefore we find Apollonius calling these Indians gods, and enrolling himself as their disciple, we have no alternative but to bring him also under the imputation under which his teachers lay. And accordingly he is introduced as saying among the so-called Naked sages of the Egyptians, the following,--I quote his very words: "

It is then not unreasonable on my part, I think, to have yielded myself to a philosophy so highly elaborated, to a philosophy which, if I may use a metaphor from the stage, the Indians mount, as it deserved to be mounted, upon a lofty and divine mechanism before they wheel it out upon the stage. And that I was right to admire them, and that I am right in considering them wise and blessed, it is now time to learn." And after a little he says : " For they are not only gods, but are adorned with all the gifts of the Pythian prophetess." And he is introduced to Domitian with these words on his lips : " What war have you with Iarchas or with Phraotes, both of them Indians, whom I consider to be the only men that are really gods and that deserve this ... appellation? " And there are other passages also in which this history of Philostratus recognises the persons above mentioned as gods and teachers of the sage, and admits him to have accepted rings from them, but now he forgets all about it, and does not see that in maligning the teachers, he maligns the disciple.

XXVIII

AND a little lower down in the book he brings a flute-player upon the stage, and he relates at length how Apollonius delivered himself with great gravity of long essays upon the different modes maker of playing the flute, as if it were the most important and clever of the sciences. And he relates how the Emperor Vespasian offered him prayers just as if he were a god, for we learn that Vespasian said in a tone of prayer: "Do thou make me Emperor," whereupon Apollonius answered: " I have made you so." What else can anyone do but loathe this utterance for its boastfulness, so nearly does it approach downright madness, for one who was the pilot of a ship in Egypt to boast of being himself a god already and a maker of kings? For Apollonius himself has informed us a little before in the course of his conversation with the Indian that his soul had previously been that of a pilot.

XXIX

AND to the same Emperor, when the latter asks him to notify to him those whom he most approved of among philosophers as advisers and counsellors of his policy, Apollonius replies in these words: " ' These gentlemen here are also good advisers in such matters,' and he pointed to Dion and to Euphrates, because he had not yet quarrelled with the latter." And again, he said, "My sovereign, Euphrates and Dion have long been known to you and they are at your door, and are much concerned for your welfare.

Summon them also therefore to your conference, for they are both of them wise." Whereupon Vespasian answered: "I throw my doors open wide to wise men." What can we think of the prescience of our hero? On this occasion Euphrates is both good and wise, because he has not yet quarrelled with him; but when he has,--and before long he is going to,--then see how the same person writes to the Emperor Domitian: " And yet if you want to know how much a philosopher may attain by flattery of the mighty you have only to look at the case of Euphrates. For in his case why do I speak of wealth from that source? Why, he has perfect fountains of wealth, and already at the banks he discusses prices as a merchant might or a huckster, or a tax-gatherer or a low money-changer; for all these roles are his if there is anything to buy or sell.

And he clings like a limpet to the doors of the mighty, and you see him standing at them more regularly than any doorkeeper would do; indeed he is often caught by the doorkeepers, just as greedy dogs might be. But he never yet bestowed a farthing on a philosopher, but he walls up all his wealth within his house; only supporting this Egyptian out of other people's money, and sharpening his tongue against me, when it ought to be cut out. However I will leave Euphrates to yourself: for unless you approve of flatterers, you will find the fellow worse than I represent him." Surely one who first bears witness to Vespasian the father that Euphrates is a wise and good man, and then inveighs against him in this style to his son, is openly convicted of praising and blaming the same person. Was it then the case that this man, who was endowed with knowledge of the future, did not know what the character of Euphrates was, nor what it was going to be ?

For it is not now the first time, but already in the case of Vespasian himself he is inclined to accuse him of being the worst of characters. How then is it that he recommended such a person to the sovereign so warmly, that in consequence of his recommendation the latter threw open wide the doors of his palace to him ? Why, is it not clear to a blind man, as they say, that in the matter of foreknowledge the fellow is traduced by his own historian; though on other ground he might be regarded as an honest man, if we could suppose that originally, and before he learned by experience, he wished to gain access to the palace as freely for his friends, Euphrates included, as for himself, but was afterwards moved by his quarrel to use such language of him.

I have no wish in thus arguing to accuse Apollonius of having falsely blamed Euphrates, who was the most distinguished philosopher of all the men of his age, so much so that his praises are still on the lips of students of philosophy. Not but what anyone who was minded to do so could take this as a palmary example of slander and back-biting and use it against Apollonius. For if Euphrates be really by their admission a leader in all philosophy, it is open to us to accuse his rival of censoriousness, when he attacks him for his monstrous conduct; and to suppose that the latter contracted his evil reputation because he was thus attacked by him for pursuing,-- that was the accusation,--a life so little satisfactory to a philosopher.

XXX

IN the sixth book our story-teller resumes his tale of miracles ; for he brings his hero, together with his companions, on camel-back to see those whom he the calls the Naked philosophers of Egypt. Here then at the bidding of one of these sages an elm-tree, we are told, spoke to Apollonius in an articulate but feminine voice, and this is the sort of thing which the Lover of Truth expects us to believe. Then he has a story of pigmies who live on the other side of their country and of man-eaters and of shadow-footed men and of a satyr whom Apollonius made drunk. From these sages Apollonius is brought back again to Hellas, where he renews his interviews and his prophesies to Titus. Then we hear about a youth who was bitten by a mad dog. He is rescued from his distress by Apollonius, who forthwith proceeds to divine whose soul it was that the dog had inside him; and we learn that it was that of Amasis, a former king of Egypt, for the sage's humanity extended to dogs.

XXXI

THESE then are the achievements which preceded his accusation, and it behoves us to notice throughout the treatise that, even if we admit the author to tell the truth in his stories of miracles, he yet clearly shows that they were severally performed by Apollonius with the co-operation of a demon. For his presentiment of the plague, though it might not seem to be magical and uncanny, if he owed it, as he himself said, to the lightness and purity of his diet, yet might quite as well have been a premonition imparted to him in intercourse with a demon. For though the other stories of his having grasped and foretold the future by virtue of his prescience can be refuted by a thousand arguments which Philostratus' own text supplies, nevertheless, if we allow this particular story to be true, I should certainly say that his apprehension of futurity was anyhow in some cases, though it was not so in all, due to some uncanny contrivance of a demon that was his familiar. This is clearly proved by the fact that he did not retain his gift of foreknowledge uniformly and in all cases; but was at fault in most cases, and had through ignorance to make enquiries, as he would not have needed to do, if he had been endowed with divine power and virtue. And the very cessation of the plague, according to the particular turn which was given to the drama, has already been shown to have been a delusion and nothing more.

Moreover, the soul of Achilles should not have been lingering about his own monument, quitting the Islands of the Blest and the places of repose, as people would probably say. In this case too it was surely a demon that appeared to Apollonius and in whose presence he found himself? Then again the licentious youth was clearly the victim of an indwelling demon; and both it and the Empusa and the Lamia which is said to have played off its mad pranks on Menippus, were probably driven out by him with the help of a more important demon; the same is true also of the youth who had been driven out of his mind by the mad dog; and the frenzied dog itself was restored to its senses by the same method. You must then, as I said, regard the whole series of miracles wrought by him, as having been accomplished through a ministry of demons; for the resuscitation of the girl must be divested of any miraculous character, if she was really alive all the time and still bore in herself a vital spark, as the author says, and if a vapour rose over her face. For it is impossible, as I said before, that such a miracle should have been passed over in silence in Rome itself, if it happened when the sovereign was close by.

XXXII

THERE are a thousand other examples then which we may select from the same books where the narrative refutes itself by its very incongruities, so enabling us to detect its mythical and miracle-mongering character. At the same time we need not devote too much attention and study to the gentleman's career, seeing that those of our contemporaries among whom his memory survives at all, are so far from classing him among divine and extraordinary and wonderful beings, that they do not even rank him among philosophers. This being so, let us be content with the remarks we have made, and proceed to consider the seventh book of his history.

XXXIII

HERE then we find him categorically accused of being a wizard. Next we find Demetrius the philosopher trying to dissuade him from going on to Rome, and Apollonius rejects his advice in words which are full of vulgar effrontery and fulsome praise of himself. They are as follows: " But I know most human affairs, seeing that I know everything; at the same time I reserve my knowledge partly for good men, partly for the wise, partly for myself, partly for the gods." And yet the man who in these words brags about his omniscience, before he goes much further is accused by the text itself of an ignorance in certain matters. Next Apollonius disguises Damis, for the latter conceals the fact of his being a philosopher because he is afraid of death. Listen then to the words in which our author apologises for him : " This was the reason then of Damis' putting off his Pythagorean dress. For he says that it was not cowardice that led him to make the change, nor regret at having worn it; but he did it because the device recommended itself as suggested by the expedience of the moment."

XXXIV

After this Philostratus sets forth four counts of the indictment which he imagines it will be easy for his hero to defend himself from, and he admits that he has collected these out of a great many others. Of these the first was: What induced him to wear a different robe from everybody else ? and the second :

Why was it that men esteemed him to be a god ? the third, How had he managed to predict the plague to the Ephesians? and last of all: In whose behoof had he gone to a certain field and cut up the Arcadian boy ? To meet these then he alleges Apollonius to have written an apology. But first of all he relates how he was cast into prison, and the miracle which he wrought there. For we hear that Damis was extremely downcast at the misfortunes which he imagined had befallen his teacher; whereupon Apollonius showed him his leg released without effort from the chain. Then having thus alleviated his follower's grief, he put his foot back again into its former condition and habit. After that he was brought to trial before the Emperor Domitian, and we read that he was acquitted on the charges, and that after being so acquitted he, wiih curious inopportuneness, as it seems to me, cried out in the court exactly as follows: " Accord me too, if you will, an opportunity to speak; but if not, then send someone to take my body, for my soul you cannot take. Nay you cannot even take my body,' for thou shalt not slay me, since I tell thee I am not mortal.'" And then after this famous utterance, we are told that he vanished from the court, and this is the conclusion of the whole drama.

XXXV

Now in regard to the miracle in the prison, which it seems was an illusion, imposed on the eyes of Damis by the familiar demon, our author adds the following remark ; " Damis says that it was then for the first time that he truly understood the nature of Apollonius, to wit that it was divine and superhuman; for without offering any sacrifice,---and how indeed in prison could he have offered one?--and without a single prayer, without even a word, he quietly laughed at the fetters, and then inserting his leg in them afresh, he comported himself like any other prisoner."

I should be the last to accuse his pupil of being a dull-witted man, because, after being with him all his life, and witnessing him work miracles by means of certain uncanny agencies, he failed to regard him as in any way superior to the rest of mortal men; but now after such a display of thaumaturgic energy as the above, he is still ignorant of his true character; and taking him to be a mere man he is full of anxiety (as in that case he might well be), and full of apprehension in his behalf, lest any affliction should come upon him against his own wish and will. But if indeed it was now for the first time, after having passed so long a time with him, that he realised that he was indeed divine, and superior to the rest of the human race, then it behoves us to scrutinize the reason which our author alleges for his doing so, in these words: " For without any sacrifice, and without a single prayer, and without uttering a single mysterious word " he saw that he had wrought this miracle.

It follows that the fellow's earlier feats were accomplished by the help of some uncanny trick, and that is why, as he says, Damis was not astounded at these things, nor filled with wonder by them. Naturally, then he now for the first time experienced these feelings, because he felt that his master had accomplished something which was quite unusual and contrary to his habitual performances. In reference however to the phantom chains shown to Damis and to his departure from the law-courts, I will quote the words which Apollonius himself addresses to Domitian.

For when the monarch ordered him to be thrown into chains, Apollonius, with perfect consistency, argued as follows: " If you think me a wizard, how will you bind me ? And if you bind me, how can you say that I am a wizard." Surely one may invert this argument and use it against him somewhat as follows, keeping to his own premisses: If you are not a wizard, then how was your leg liberated from the chains? And if it was liberated, then how are you not a wizard? And if, because he submits to the chains, he is not a wizard, then if he does not submit to them, he is a wizard by his own admission. And again if, because he submitted to be brought to trial, he was not a wizard, he was yet clearly revealed as such when he ran off and eluded the court and retinue of the Emperor, I mean of course the bodyguard that stood round him. Now I believe that our author is aware of this, and endeavours to gloze over the fact, when he pretends that this miracle was exhibited without sacrifice or any sort of incantation by some ineffable and superhuman power.

XXXVI

MOREOVER we have not got to go far, before a fresh test of his character is supplied to us ; for presently a messenger presents himself and says: " O Apollonius, the Emperor releases you from these chains, and permits you to reside in the jail where prisoners are not bound " ; whereupon Apollonius, who is superior to mankind and has foreknowledge of what is coming, and according to the poet

"Hath understanding of the dumb and heareth him who speaks not"

is so overjoyed., as well he might be, at the news, that he suddenly drops out of his gift of foreknowledge, and asks outright : " Who then will get me out of this place ? " and the messenger replied : " I myself, so follow me."

XXXVII

NEXT this most divine of men composes in the most careful of manners an harangue in defence of himself, quite unaware that after all his composition would prove a mere waste of effort. For he imagines that the Emperor will listen to his defence of his case, and on that assumption he arranges his apology along extremely plausible lines; but the latter, by refusing to wait, renders all his trouble useless and unnecessary. I would ask you then to listen to the following, for what he says is a refutation of himself: "But inasmuch as he had composed an oration which he meant to deliver in defence of himself by the clock, only the tyrant confined him to the questions which I have enumerated, I have determined to publish this oration also." Note then how utterly at fault this entirely divinest of beings was about the future, if he took so much trouble and care to proportion the length of his apology to the time allowed him by the water-clock.

XXXVIII

BUT we must not omit to pass in review the defence which he so vainly composed, for it contains among many examples of the arrogance with which he addressed Domitian, the following utterance, to wit, when he says " as Vespasian made you Emperor, so I made him." Heavens, what braggadocio! No ordinary person anyhow, nor any real philosopher either, transcending the rest of mankind, could indulge in such high-faluting bombast without exposing himself in the eyes of sensible men to a charge of being mad. Next in trying to rid himself of the suspicion which weighed upon him, he holds the following language concerning magicians and wizards; " But I call wizards men of false wisdom, for with them the unreal is made real, and the real becomes incredible." One may learn then from the whole treatise and from the particular episodes set forth therein, whether we ought to rank him among divine and philosophic men or among wizards.

We have only to observe what he himself has said about wizards and falsely wise men together with what is published in his own history. For when oak trees and elms talk in articulate and feminine tones, and tripods move of their own accord, and waiters of copper serve at table, and jars are filled with showers and with winds, and water of sandarac and all the other things of the kind are introduced among those whom he accounted gods and also did not hesitate to entitle his teachers, of whom else are all these things characteristic, except of people who can exhibit "the unreal as real and the real as incredible "? In himself calling the latter wizards, he shows that they are people whose wisdom is false. Is it then on the strength of these things that this divine man, endowed with all virtue and the darling of the gods, is to bind on his brow the prize of wisdom, and to be accounted truly more divine than Pythagoras and his successors, and to be considered far more blessed than he; is he not rather to be found guilty of false wisdom and carry off the first prize for wretches?

XXXIX

IN the same book we are told that he had reasoned in Ionia about the power of the Fates, and had taught that the threads they spin are so immutable that, if they decree a kingdom to another which already belongs to some one, then, even if that other were slain by the possessor for fear lest he should ever have it taken away by him, the latter would yet be raised from the dead and live again in fulfilment of the decrees of the Fates ; and he continues in these very words: "He who is destined to become a carpenter, will become one, even though his hands have been cut off; and he who has been predestined to carry off the prize for running in the Olympic games, will never fail to win, even though he break his leg; and the man to whom the Fates have decreed that he shall be an eminent archer, will not miss the mark, even though he lose his eyesight." And then by way of flattering the sovereign he adds the following : " And in drawing my examples from royalty, I had reference, I admit, to the Acrisii and to the house of Laius, and to Astyages, the Mede, and to many other monarchs who thought that their power was well established, and of whom some were supposed to have slain their own children and others their descendants, yet were deprived by them of their thrones, when they grew up and issued forth against them out of obscurity in accordance with destiny.

Well, if I were inclined to flattery I should have said that I had your own history in my mind, when you were blockaded by Vitellius, and the temple of Jupiter was burnt on the brow of the hill, overlooking the city. And Vitellius declared that his own fortune was assured, so long as you did not escape him, although you were at the time quite a stripling, and not the man you are now. And yet because the Fates had decreed otherwise, he perished with all his counsels, while you are now in possession of his throne. However, since I abhor the forced concords of flattery, for it seems to me that they are everything that is out of time and out of tune, let me at once cut this string out of my lyre, and request you to consider that on that occasion I had not your fortunes in my mind." In this passage, a treatise written ostensibly in the interest of truth draws a picture of a man who was at once a flatterer and a liar, and anything rather than a philosopher; for after inveighing so bitterly on the earlier occasion against Domitian, he now flatters him, generous fellow that he is, and pretends that the doctrines he mooted in Ionia about the Fates and Necessity, so far from being directed against him rather told in his favour.

Take then your history, my author, and regaining your sobriety after, your fit of drunkenness, read out loud and in a truth-loving tone the passages you wrote on a former occasion, without concealing anything; read how when he was staying in Ephesus he did his best "to alienate his friends from Domitian, and encouraged them to espouse the cause of the safety of all, and as it occurred to him that intercourse with them by letter was dangerous to them, he would take now one and now another of the most discreet of his own companions aside and say to them : ' I have a most important secret business to entrust to yourselves, so you must betake yourself to Rome to such and such persons, and converse with them !' " And of how " he delivered a discourse on the subject of the Fates and Necessity. and argued that not even tyrants can overpower the decrees of the Fates." And how "directing the attention of his audience to a brazen statue of Domitian which stood close by that of the Meles, he said : ' Thou fool, how much art thou mistaken in thy views of Necessity and of the Fates.

For even if thou shouldst slay the man who is fated to be despot after thyself, he shall corne to life again.' " The man then who, after holding such language as this, proceeds to flatter the tyrant, and cynically pretends that none of this language was directed against him, how can we judge him other than capable of all villainy and meanness ; unless indeed you assume that the authors who have handed down to us these details of him were lying fellows who meant to accuse their hero and not true historians ? But in that case what becomes, to use the language of the Lover of Truth, of those who " were historians at once most highly educated and respectful of the truth, namely Damis the philosopher who even lived with the man in question and Philostratus the Athenian?" For these are the authors who lay these facts before us, and they are clearly convicted by the light of truth, since they thus contradict themselves, of being vapouring braggarts and nothing else, convicted by their inconsistencies of being downright liars, men devoid of education and charlatans.

XL

THE story proceeds to tell us that after all this, Apollonius, liberated from the court, made up his mind to descend into the cave of Trophonius in Lebadea; but the people there would not allow him to do so, because they too regarded him as a wizard.

Surely it is legitimate in us to be puzzled, when one compares what one reads at the beginning of the book of Philostratus, I mean the passage where he owns that he is puzzled at people having regarded his hero as a wizard, and expresses his surprise at the circumstance, remarking withal, that "although Empedocles and Pythagoras and Democritus had consorted with the same Magi without ever stooping to the magic art, and Plato had derived much from the priests and prophets in Egypt, and had mingled their ideas with his own discourses, without ever being held by anyone to be a magician, yet men so far had failed to recognise his hero as one inspired by the purest wisdom, but had long since accounted him a magician and still did so, because he had consorted with the Magi of Babylon and the Brahmans of India, and the Naked sages of Egypt." XL What answer then can we make to him, except this ?-- My good fellow, what was your hero up to in this line, for him alone to have been regarded both long ago and now as a wizard in contrast with these great men; who though, as you admit, they had made trial of the same teachers as he, yet were eminent both in the age in which thev nourished, and also bequeathed to posterity in their philosophy a gift of such excellence that its praises are still sung.

Is such a contrast possible, unless he was caught by men of good sense meddling with things that were unlawful? There are still among our contemporaries those who say that they have found superstitious devices dedicated in the name of this man; though I admit I have no wish to pay attention to them.

However as regards his death, although Philostratus follows in his book the accounts of earlier writers, he declares that he knows nothing of the truth; for he says that people in Ephesus related that Apollonius died there, while others said that he died in Lindus after entering the temple of Athene, and others in Crete; and after shedding so much doubt on the manner of his end, he yet inclines to believe that he went to heaven body and all. For he says that after he had run into the temple, the gates were closed and a strange hymn of maidens was heard to issue from the building, and the words of their song were: " Come, come, to heaven, come." But he says that he had never come across any sepulchre or "cenotaph of his hero, although he had visited the greater part of the whole earth; but what he would like us to believe is that his hero never encountered death at all, for on a former occasion when he is canvassing the manner in which he died, he adds the proviso: " If he did die." But in a later passage he declares in so many words that he went to heaven. This is why he avows, no less in the exordium of his book than throughout it, that it was by reason of his being such as he was that he wooed philosophy in a diviner manner than Pythagoras and Empedocles.

XLI

ALTHOUGH then the limits of our discourse are reached in the above, I would yet, if you will allow me, raise a few points in connexion with the Fates and with destiny, in order to ascertain what aim his work has in view, when throughout its argument it sets itself to demolish our responsibility, and to substitute for it necessity, and destiny and the Fates.

For in this way we shall finally and completely refute the tenets professed by the author and prove their falsity. If then, according to the views of true philosophy, every soul is immortal, for that which is perpetually moving is immortal, whereas that which moves another, and is itself moved by others, in admitting a cessation of its own movement, admits a cessation of life ; and if responsibility depends on personal choice, and God is not responsible, then what reason is there for concluding that the nature, which is ever in movement, is actuated against its will, and not rather in accordance with its own choice and ' decision ; for otherwise it would resemble a lifeless body in being moved by some outside agency, and would be as it were a puppet pulled by strings hither and thither.

The nature which ever moves itself would, on such ail hypothesis, effect nothing of its own initiative and movement, nor could it refer to itself the responsibility of its actions." In such a case, when it reasoned of truth it would surely not be worthy of praise ; nor on the other hand be blameworthy, because it was filled with vice and wickedness ? Why then, I would ask you, my good fellow, do you revile Euphrates and find fault with him, if it is not of his own initiative, but by the force of destiny, that he devoted himself to gain, as you pretend, and neglected the philosophical ideal? And why do you insult wizards, by calling them false sophists, if they are dragged down by the Fates, as you believe, to their miserable life ? And why do you keep in your vocabulary at all such a word as vice, when any evil man is unjustly condemned by you, since it is by necessity that he fulfils his destined term? And again on what principle do you solemnly enroll yourself a disciple of the wonderful teacher Pythagoras, and insist on praising one who, instead of being a lover of philosophy, was a mere toy in the hands of the Fates ? And as for Phraotes and Iarchas, the philosophers of the Indians, what have they done to win from you the reputation of being gods, unless the glory they acquired by their culture and virtue was their own? And in the same way with regard to Nero and Domitian, why do you not saddle upon the Fates and on Necessity the responsibility for their unbridled insolence, and acquit them of all responsibility and blame?

But if as you say a man who is destined to be a runner, or an archer or a carpenter, cannot avoid being so, surely also if it has been destined that a man should be a wizard, and that being his character, a magician or a murderer and a wicked man and a reprobate, come what will, he must of necessity end by being such a person. Why then do you go wandering about, preaching the virtues to those who are incapable of reform? Why do you blame those who are the monsters they are, not of their own choice, but by predestination? And why too, if it was decreed by fate that you yourself being of a divine nature should transcend the glory of kings, did you visit schools of teachers and philosophers, and trouble yourself about Arabians and about the Magi of Babylon, and the wise men of India? For in any case surely, even without your holding communications with them, the decrees of the Fates were bound to be fulfilled in your case.

And why do you vainly cast before those whom you consider to be gods, your honey-cake and your frankincense, and putting on the cloak of religion encourage your companions to be diligent at their prayers? And what do you yourself in your prayers ask of the gods, inasmuch as you admit that they too are subject to Destiny? Nay you ought to make a clean sweep of all the other gods, and sacrifice to Necessity alone and to the Fates, and pay your respects rather to Destiny than to Zeus himself. In that case no doubt you would have no gods left; and rightly too, seeing that they are not even able to help mankind. And again, if it were decreed by fate that the citizens of Ephesus should be afflicted with pestilence, why did you sanction the opposite and so try to thwart destiny ? Nay, why did you dare to transcend destiny, and as it were raise a trophy over her

? And again in the case of the maiden raised to life, the thread of Clotho had reached its limit, and that being so why did you, when she was dead, bind a fresh thread on the spindle, by coming forward yourself in the role of the saviour of her life ?

But perhaps you will say the Fates drove you also on to these courses. Yet you cannot say that they did so out of respect to your merits; far from it, seeing that before you passed into this body of yours, you were yourself, by your own account, a sea-faring man who spent his life upon the waves, and that of necessity, for even this could not have been otherwise. There is therefore nothing remarkable about your earliest birth, or your upbringing, or your education in the circle of arts, or in your wise self-discipline in the prime of your life, or of your training. In philosophy; for it was after all some necessity of the Fates that led you to Babylon, and you were as it were driven on to associate with the sages of India; and it was not your own will and choice, nor a love of philosophy either, but Fate that led you in her noose to the Naked sages of the Egyptians, and to Gadeira and to the pillars of Hercules ; and it was she who forced you to wander about the eastern and western oceans, and along with her spindles whirled you idly around.

But if anyone admits, as they must, that his endowment with wisdom was due to these causes, then it was destiny that was responsible for them; and we must no longer reckon your hero among those who are fond of learning, nor can we with any pretence of reason admire a philosophy which was provided, not intentionally, but by necessity, for him. And we shall have to class on one and the same level, according to him, Pythagoras himself with any pretentious and abject slave, and Socrates himself, who died in behalf of philosophy with those who accused him and clamoured for his death. Diogenes, too, with the golden youth of Athens; and, to sum up, the wisest man will not differ from the most imprudent, nor the unjustest from the justest, nor the most abandoned from the most temperate, nor the worst of cowards from the greatest of heroes; for they have all been demonstrated to be playthings of destiny and of the Fates.

XLII

HOWEVER, the herald of truth will raise his voice against such arguments, and say: O ye men, mortal and perishable race, whither are you drifting, after drinking the unmixed cup of ignorance? Be done with it at last, wake up and be sober; and, raising the eyes of your intelligence, gaze upon the august countenance of truth. It is not lawful for truth to be in conflict and contradiction with herself; nor that of two pronounced opposites there should exist but one and the same ground and cause.

The universe is ordered by the divine laws of the providence of God that controls all things, and the peculiar nature of man's soul renders him master of himself and judge, ruler and lord of himself; and it teaches him through the laws of nature, and the tenets of philosophy, that of things which exist some are within our own control, but others not; and within our control is everything which comes into being in accordance with our will and choice and action, and these are naturally free, unhindered and unimpeded. But such things as are not in our control are weak and servile, restrained and alien to ourselves; for example, our bodily processes and external objects which are both lifeless and destitute of reason, and in their manner of existence wholly foreign to the proper nature of a reasonable living creature.

As for things which are in our control, each one of us possesses in the will itself alternative impulses of virtue and vice; and while the principle which controls the universe and governs it executes its rounds in direct accordance with nature, it is at the same time always accompanied by a justice which punishes infractions of the divine law; but for the motives on which we act the responsibility lies not with destiny nor fate, nor with necessity. It lies with him who makes the choice, and God is not to be blamed.

If therefore anyone is so foolhardy as to controvert the fact of our responsibility, let him be duly exposed; and let him openly proclaim that lie is an atheist, seeing that he does not recognise either providence or God or anything else except the Fates and necessity. And let him bare-headed enumerate the consequences of these doctrines, let him cease to call anyone wise or foolish, just or unjust, virtuous or vicious, or charlatan; let him deny that anyone is divine in our humanity, that there is any philosophy, any education, in a word any art of any kind, or science, let him not call anyone else by nature good or evil, but admit that everything whatever is whirled round in an eddy of necessity by the spindles of the Fates.

Let such a person then be registered as an atheist and impious man in the tribunal of the pious and of philosophers. And if anyone under the cloak of other opinions undertakes to entertain ideas of Providence and of the gods, yet, in addition to these champions the cause of Destiny and Fate, so upholding conflicting and opposed opinions, let him be classed among the senseless and condemned to pay the penalty of his folly. This then is so. But if after this there still remain those who are disposed to register this man's name in the schools of philosophers, it shall be said that, even if they succeed in clearing him from the filth thrown by others, nay in disentangling him from the pinchbeck properties in which the author of this book has wheeled him in upon the stage, we shall raise no objection to their doing so.

At the same time if anyone ventures to overpass the limits of truth and tries to deify him as no other philosopher has been deified, he will at the best, though unawares, be rubbing into him the accusation of wizardry; for this work of pretentious sophistry can only serve, in my opinion, to convict him, and lay him open in the eyes of all men of sense to this terrible accusation.

For more esoteric books please, visit our web site
http://www.andras-nagy.com

Other book about Apollonius

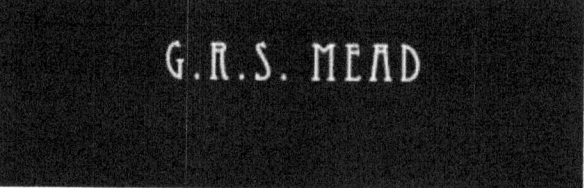

Publised by Ancient Wisdom Publications (formerly Murine Press)
ISBN 13   9781441413826

Made in the USA
Columbia, SC
17 July 2020